PHP

MG MARTIN

TABLE OF CONTENTS

PHP: *Basic Fundamental Guide for Beginners* 1

Introduction to PHP 3

Chapter 1: Starting Up and Running With PHP..................................4

Chapter 2: A Walk Through the PHP Language 10

Chapter 3: PHP Form Handling 35

Chapter 4: Introduction Databases and SQL 39

Chapter 5: Manipulate MySQL Data With PHP..................................49

Chapter 6: PHP Sessions, Cookies, and Authentication....................66

Conclusion..71

PHP: *A Comprehensive Intermediate Guide to Learn the Concept of PHP Programming* 73

Introduction 75

Chapter 1: All about PHP 76

Chapter 2: Restful APIs 82

Chapter 3: PHP and Internet Services...95

Chapter 4: PHP Graphics..106

Chapter 5: Classes and Objects...112

Chapter 6: Security and Encryption.................................. 119

Chapter 7: Regular Expressions 126

Chapter 8: Files... 135

Chapter 9: Session and Cookies 142

Chapter 10: Advanced OOP.. 147

Conclusion 153

PHP: *Advanced Detailed Approach to Master PHP Programming Language for Web Development* **155**

Introduction... 157

Chapter 1: Styles of Coding in PHP................................. 158

Chapter 2: Object-Oriented Programming using Design Patterns. 179

Chapter 3: Handling Errors 200

Chapter 4: Running PHP-Templates and the Web 215

Chapter 5: PHP Standalone Scripts................................. 223

Chapter 6: Controlling the Development Environment 225

Chapter 7: Designing a Great API 228

Conclusion 231

Description 232

PHP

Basic Fundamental Guide for Beginners

Introduction to PHP

Is this your first time to code in PHP? Are you stuck in the MySQL database? Perhaps you don't know how to create sessions or cookies in PHP? This book will take you through a complete step-by-step process of learning PHP. Whether you have just started or you want to continue from where you left, get this masterpiece containing the fundamental concepts of PHP.

Besides that, we will explain everything in a friendly and interactive manner to make sure that you understand every concept. We will also provide you with screenshots of source code to type in your favorite text editor.

If your goal is to become a great PHP developer, then this book is for you. If you want to quickly master the basic fundamentals of PHP programming, then this book will help you do so. If you are tired of debugging your code and you want to learn how you can fix it up fast, then we have the solution for you.

PHP is an amazing language with easy-to-understand concepts. If you can learn PHP today, then you will manage to create anything from a simple contact form to a complete web application. You will even learn how to create a mailing list or a content management system.

That said, this book will teach you how to do that. We will also teach you how to build PHP applications to solve real-world problems. Since PHP is a web-based language, a little knowledge of HTML and CSS will help you. Still, if you're green on HTML and CSS. Don't worry, HTML and CSS are just easy as 1, 2, and 3.

3

Chapter 1

Starting Up and Running With PHP

Introduction to PHP

Welcome to PHP. A popular programming language used by many people across the world.

PHP is an amazing language which you can use to build interactive and dynamic websites. When you are done writing your PHP program, you must have a Web server to run your code. PHP programs serve web pages to visitors based on their request. Put simply, it is a server side language. PHP has one prominent feature where you can embed your written code within the pages of HTML. This makes it very easy for anyone who wants to make dynamic content.

In the previous paragraph, you can simply say I described PHP as 'interactive and dynamic.'

As a beginner to PHP programming, you may be wondering about what exactly those two phrases mean. To save you time, when you hear a programmer describe a web page as being dynamic, they are simply trying to say that the contents of the page change automatically whenever the page is viewed. You can compare this with a static HTML file which never changes no matter how many people visit the page. Meanwhile, an interactive web page is one which accepts and responds to the input it receives from the visitors. A good example of an interactive website is a web forum. In a web forum, different users can post a message which is then displayed on the forum for everyone to see.

If you have been wondering what PHP stands for, then you are in the right place. PHP is an abbreviation for Hypertext Preprocessor. By just knowing the full meaning of PHP, you can begin to tell some of the capabilities of the language. In simple terms, it processes information and unveils it as hypertext. Many developers prefer recursive acronyms and PHP is very appealing to developers.

In PHP, for you to see the results after you have written your code, you must run your program on a PHP server. Below are the steps to follow if you want to run your PHP program on a Web server:

1. First, a visitor will make a request for a web page by either typing the URL of the webpage or clicking on a link. The visitor can send data to the web server as well with the help of a form attached to the web page.

2. The server finds out which type of request it is, once it knows that the language is PHP. It begins processing the request.

3. Once the processing is completed, the visitor sees a page.

The most exciting thing takes place when the PHP program runs. Since PHP is a very flexible language, a single PHP script can perform a multitude of interesting tasks. Some of the tasks it can perform are:

- Process details in a form

- Read and write files on a web server

- It can process data kept in a web server which has a database

- Build dynamic graphics

Lastly, when any of the above tasks are done, a PHP script can show a customized HTML web page to the visitor.

Why should I use PHP?

Most people new to PHP always ask this question. If you happen to be among them, here is something interesting for you, many internet service providers and web hosting firms have systems that are compatible with PHP. Today, a big population of developers use PHP, and they are very many because a majority of the websites are built on PHP programming.

Another powerful feature that you will get, if you choose to use the PHP language, is that it's cross-platform compatible. What this one simply means is that you can run your PHP programs on more than one platform. It doesn't matter if the platform you're using is Mac OS X, Windows, FreeBSD, and Solaris. Plus, the PHP engine is compatible with some of the popular web servers like Internet Information Server, Zeus, Apache, and lighttpd. This implies that if you want to develop your PHP program in, let's say, a Windows setup and later deploy it on Mac OS X, it is possible. In addition, the process of migrating your entire PHP program is easy. No stress involved.

Now, before we begin to discuss the basics of PHP language. I want to briefly show you the steps in setting up your PHP environment. Then, you can learn how to write a simple PHP code.

First PHP Code

What you should have

For you to actually run your first PHP script, you have to install and run a PHP Web server. You can pick any of the choices below:

- **Run localhost on your computer**

In this option, you will be running PHP on your computer. In other words, you will install a local PHP Web server on your machine. The easiest way you can achieve this is by looking online for a complete package. XAMPP is one of the best choices you should go for. This comes with the Apache Web server, MySQL database engine, PHP, and many other applications. No stress when it comes to the installation. Just a click of a button and you'll be done.

- **Run your coded scripts on a web host**

Now, if you have an active web hosting account which is designed to allow PHP, you can run your PHP scripts there. What you will do is use the FTP to upload your scripts. If you upload everything, then you can run the server to see the results. The disadvantage with a web server is that it is not fast compared to a local host.

Your First Script

Below is a script of PHP that you will learn how to create.

```
<Code />

<!DOCTYPE html PUBLIC "-//W3C//DTD XHTML 1.0 Strict//EN"
    "http://www.w3.org/TR/xhtml1/DTD/xhtml1-strict.dtd">
<html xmlns="http://www.w3.org/1999/xhtml" xml:lang="en" lang="en">
    <head>
      <title>My first PHP script</title>
    </head>
    <body>
      <p><?php echo "Hello, world!"; ?></p>
    </body>
</html>
```

In the above script, the majority is made up of XHTML.

So, the <? Php and ?> tags pass a message to the Web server that everything in the tags is a PHP code. The line of code enclosed within the PHP tags is simple. It makes use of a built-in function called 'echo,' which prints a simple text ("Hello, world!") on the website. The PHP language has a lot of functions which we are going to learn in the following chapters. These functions are important to help a developer or programmer build applications.

7

You should pay attention to the semicolon (;) immediately after the line of PHP. The semicolon shows the end of the PHP line of code. Every time you finish writing your line of PHP, you should put a semicolon. However, if you are writing a single line of code like in the example above, then it is optional. You can choose to put it in or ignore it. But, not when you have more than one line of PHP script.

Creating the PHP script

Now, for you to create a similar script like the one above, first, you must get a text editor. Nowadays, many computers have their own text editors such as:

- Windows notepad and the text editor for the MAC

However, if you feel like the above options are not the best for you, then you can choose to download Sublime text. Once you have your text editor ready, you should type the code below in the editor. Save it in any name but make sure you store in the pathway of your web server:

```
<html>
<head>
 <title>PHP Test</title>
</head>
<body>
<?php echo '<p>Hello World</p>'; ?>
</body>
</html>
```

However, if you have a web hosting account, use FTP to upload your code before you run it.

Test the script

We will now assume that you have done everything outlined above. The only thing remaining is to run your script. If you want to run your script, enter the following URLs into your web address:

- http://localhost/hello.php

8

For those who are working on an internet hosting account. Your code will resemble:

- http://www.youurl.com/hello.php

If everything runs well, then this is the output which you should get:

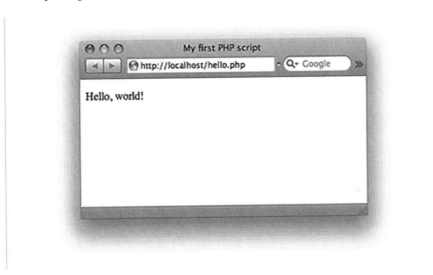

Problems?

If you encountered problems along the way while running your PHP script, you may need to go back and assess your Web server. It could be that your Web server isn't set up correctly. If for example, if the PHP code was shown on the browser instead of something similar to the above image, then that means your web server was configured well.

Next?

If the above web page displayed, congratulations! You can now write, save, and run your PHP program. You will improve the skills mentioned above in the next chapters. But for now, we are going to teach you the core basics of the PHP programming language.

Chapter 2

A Walk Through the PHP Language

At this point, you have now learned what PHP is and what some of its uses are. I believe you that you were able to run your first PHP program. Now, in this chapter, we are going to help you learn more about the core basics of PHP. This chapter will focus on:

- Variables

- PHP operators

- Constants

- Data types and many others

Variables in PHP

One of the most important things in any programming language is variables. A variable can be described as a container which can carry certain values. With variables, some values can change in the process of execution. And it's this ability to manage dynamic values which makes the variables so powerful in programming.

For instance, let's look at this line of PHP code:

echo 4 + 4;

As you might predict, this script will print 8 when it's executed. This is beautiful, but let's say, you want to show the value of 3+ 4. The only way out is to write the code like the one shown below:

echo 3 + 4;

Now, this is when variables become useful. If you decide to use variables rather than numbers in your code, then your script becomes more flexible and useful. Here is an example to show you how variables can be used:

Echo $a + $b;

The line of code above is general. But, it gives you much flexibility because you can assign any numbers to variables *$a* and *$b*. In its current state, if you were to execute this code, it will show you the sum of the values of *$a* and *$b*.

$a=4;

$b=3;

Echo $a + $b;

Naming variables

A variable is made of two parts. Those two parts consist of the variable name together with the value the variable carries. A good practice when it comes to naming your variables is to use names which are familiar to the task or operation performed. Similar to other programming languages, there are rules one must follow when giving names to variables:

- Variable names should have the dollar sign at the start

- After the dollar sign, a letter or underscore is permitted

Another important point which you need to remember is PHP variable names are case-sensitive. This means if you write *$Variable* and later write *$variable*, they are all different. I will suggest you pick one method which you will use to write all your variables and stick to that method. If you can do this, then you will avoid confusion. Again, while the length

11

of a variable is not fixed, it is good to note that having a variable name with more than 30 characters looks abnormal. If you want to see what variables look like in PHP, then here is an example:

- *$_342*

- *$my_variable*

- *$y*

- *$number*

Declaring a variable

Declaring a PHP variable is what many developers call 'creating a variable.' To declare a variable is not something hard to do because it's very easy. For example:

$my_second_variable;

If PHP recognizes a variable's name in the code, it immediately declares the variable.

Any time you declare a variable in PHP, it's recommended that you assign the variable a value. This procedure of allocating a value to your variable is called 'initializing.' Doing this has many advantages. For example, if someone else passes through your code, they would be able to tell what type of value the variable holds. If you fail to initialize a variable, then the default value assigned is null. Have a look at how you can declare and initialize a PHP variable by trying this example:

$money=200;

Types of PHP data

All data types kept in PHP variables come in either one of the eight basic types. In the PHP language, there are four scalar data types. Data is said to be scalar if it contains just a single value. Below is a list of these data types:

- **Integer**

- **Float**

It is a floating point number like 9.34

- **String**

Consists of a series of characters such as 'How much?'

- **Boolean**

This can either be false or true

Besides the scalar types, PHP also has what we call 'compound data' types. A data type is said to be compound if it can have more than one value. Listed below are the compound data types found in PHP:

- **Array**

Represents an ordered map that has numbers or names linked to values

- **Object**

One that may have methods and properties

Lastly, PHP also has special data types. They are special since they neither contain compound or scalar data. However, they have a unique meaning:

- **Resource**

- **Null**

It might have null as the value. This means the variable does not hold any value

PHP loose typing

Something else that you need to understand about PHP is it is a loosely-typed language. In other words, it is a language which does not care about the type of data kept in a variable. What this means is that it automatically changes the variable's data type. For example, you can initialize a variable as a double integer, but add a string value to it. This is not something you can do with other programming languages like Java, which is strongly-typed.

This feature of PHP is both negative and positive. It gives you the flexibility important in different situations, but on the other hand, you will not be notified if you happen to pass a wrong data type. You will not be notified of an error, but you may notice that the output of your code is not what you expected. The good news is that PHP has a way to test this.

Expressions and Operators

Now, I believe you that you are already knowledgeable about the PHP variables, right? If somebody asks you to declare and initialize an integer variable, you are capable of doing it, right? But, programming could look dull if this is only what you could achieve with variables. This is when operators bring in a new flavor. Operators allow you to play around with the data stored in the variables so that you can come up with a new value. Take, for example, the code below. It uses the operator (-) to subtract the values of $a and $b to produce a new value:

- *echo $a-$b;*

In short, if you are still wondering what an operator is, it is a symbol with the ability to change one or more values, often resulting in a new value. On the other hand, an expression is anything which will translate into a value. This can consist of different combinations of functions, operators, variables, and values. In the previous example, *$a-$b* is an expression. Some other examples of expressions are:

- *$x - $y*

- *True*

- *$x + $y + $t*

Operands are the values and variables used together with an operator.

Types of operators

There are 10 types of operators in PHP. They are:

- **Arithmetic operators**

These include addition, subtraction, multiplication, division, and modulus

- **Assignment operators (=)**

You have already seen its application

- **Bitwise operators**

- **Comparison operators**

This lets you make comparisons between one operand and the other one in different ways.

Here's a list of the comparison operators in PHP:

Operator	Example	Result
== (equal)	$x == $y	true if $x equals $y; false otherwise
!= or <> (not equal)	$x != $y	true if $x does not equal $y; false otherwise
=== (identical)	$x === $y	true if $x equals $y and they are of the same type; false otherwise
!== (not identical)	$x !== $y	true if $x does not equal $y or they are not of the same type; false otherwise
< (less than)	$x < $y	true if $x is less than $y; false otherwise
> (greater than)	$x > $y	true if $x is greater than $y; false otherwise
<= (less than or equal to)	$x <= $y	true if $x is less than or equal to $y; false otherwise
>= (greater than or equal to)	$x >= $y	true if $x is greater than or equal to $y; false otherwise

- **Incrementing and decrementing operators**

Usually used to subtract or add the value one over and over again

- **Logical operators**

These work on the Boolean values. A Boolean value can either be true or false

- **String operators**

PHP has only one string operator which is the concatenation operator or the (dot). What this string operator does is to join two strings to make them longer.

Operator precedence

When dealing with a simple expression such as 4 + 9, it is very easy. Add 4 and 9 to get 13. But, let's examine a case where we have more than one operator, do you think we shall work it out the same way we did above? No! This is when operator precedence comes in to help. All

16

operators in PHP have been ordered based on precedence. This means that an operator with higher precedence is always executed first before one which has a lower precedence. Below is a list of operators arranged according to precedence.

Precedence of Some PHP Operators (Highest First)
++ -- (increment/decrement)
(int) (float) (string) (array) (object) (bool) (casting)
! (not)
* / % (arithmetic)
+ - . (arithmetic)
< <= > >= <> (comparison)
== != === !== (comparison)
&& (and)
|| (or)
= += -= *= /= .= %= (assignment)
and
xor
or

Constants

PHP also allows you to define constants to hold values. One thing about the values of constants is that it remains the same. In addition, constants are defined once in a PHP script.

Don't confuse constants with variables in PHP. Constants are different from variables in the way they are defined, and they don't begin with the dollar sign. However, I will recommend that you make it a habit to define all your constants in uppercase letters. In addition, don't use reserved PHP keywords to define constants. If you do so, you may confuse PHP.

Decisions and Loops

Up to this point, you have learned some of the basics of PHP. You know the number of data types in PHP, and you know the types of expressions in PHP as well as variables, right? All of the codes you have seen are categorized as a linear type of code. But, things become even interesting when you begin to use decisions and loops.

Simply put, a decision will allow you to either execute a given section of code or not depending on the results of a given test. Loops will permit the code to run repeatedly until that point when the code accomplishes a specific condition.

By integrating decisions and loops into your code, you will gain much control over your code, and you can make them dynamic. With the help of decisions and loops, you have a chance to display different kinds of content to your visitors depending on what buttons they click or where they live, among other conditions.

Making decisions

Similar to other popular programming languages, PHP gives you the power to write a code which can make a decision, depending on the current result of an expression. With 'decisions,' you have the ability to develop complex codes.

Decisions with 'If statements'

This is the easiest decision statement that one can understand. The basic nature of the 'if statement' is as follows:

If (expression) {

// put here your code

}

// additional code goes here

18

In this example, the code in the braces is executed only if the expression in the parenthesis is true.

Now, let's say the code is false, then that means the code in the braces will not be executed. However, it is important to highlight that any script after the closing brace will always be executed no matter the results of the test. So in the previous example, if the expression is true, then both the 'put here your code' and the 'additional code goes here' will run. But, if the expression is found to be false, then the 'put here your code' will not be executed, but the extra 'additional code goes here' will still be executed.

Another 'else statement'

You have seen that the 'if statement' will let you execute a code if an expression is true. But, if the expression is read as false, then the piece of code is skipped. Now, with an else statement, it gives you the ability to improve the decision-making process. Let's look at an example:

If ($z >=20) {

echo "Z is greater than twenty";

} else {

echo "Z is less than 20";

}

If $z is greater than or equal to twenty, then 'Z is greater than twenty' is displayed. However, if $Z is less than twenty, then 'Z is less than 20' is shown to the user. It is still possible to create a combination of a 'last else' statement with another 'if' statement, so you have plenty of alternative choices. PHP still offers you with a special 'else, if' in which you can combine an 'else' and 'if' statement. So you can have it like this:

```
If (expression1) {

echo "Write your statement here";

} else if (expression2) {

echo "Write your second statement here";

} else {

echo "write your last statement here";

}
```

Switch statement

There are times when you will face a scenario where you want to test an expression against many different values, each having its own assigned task if the value matches. Have a look at this example that applies to the 'if,' 'else, if' and 'else' statements:

```
If ($x === "open") {

// Open the file

} else if ($x == "save") {

// Save the file

} else if ($x == "logout") {

// logout the user

} else {

Print "Kindly select an option";

}
```

The above example repeatedly compares the same variable with different values. Well, this is very tiresome. What if you want to have a different expression?

If you were to implement it with the PHP switch statement, things just get easier and fun. The switch statement makes things look simple and elaborate. You will use the expression 'once.' You can look at the example so that you can understand what I am saying:

Switch ($X) {

case "open":

//Open your file

break;

case "save":

// save your file

break;

case "logout":

//logout the user

break;

default:

print "kindly select an option";

}

You can see that despite the second example requiring additional lines of code, it is a clear approach that is easy to follow and maintain.

Using the ternary operator

We already looked at operators in the previous sections, has and there is another operator known as the ternary operator. The ternary operator has the question mark as its symbol. Furthermore, the ternary operator evaluates three expressions:

(expression 1)? expression2: expression3;

The ternary operator is somehow similar to the 'if, else' construct. You can think of the ternary operator as a compact version of the 'if, else' style. The previous code can be interpreted like this: 'If the *expression1* is true, then the entire expression is equal to *expression1on2*, but if the *expression1* is evaluated as false, then the overall expression is equal to *expression1on3.*"

Using loops to do repeated tasks

I hope you have learned how you can make decisions with a separate snippet of code based on a written condition. Now, I want to introduce to you something more powerful. I know you have heard of the word loop. As the name suggests, there is an act of repetition in a loop. So, a loop repeats a given task until a condition is attained. Similar to decisions, the condition in a 'loop' has to be in the form of an expression. For those of you who don't understand this, let me explain it to you. If the expression is going to be false, then the loop will stop. But, as long as it is true, the loop continues to run.

While loops

This is the easiest type of loop that anyone can understand. A 'while' loop looks similar to the 'if' statement. Here is a 'while' construct:

While (expression) {

//Code

}

// More code

Looks simple, doesn't it? If the expression found in the parenthesis is evaluated and found to be true, the block of code in the braces is executed. Again, if the expression is evaluated and found to be true, then the block of code is executed again, and the pattern goes on. However, let's say the expression is false, what happens? The loop exits the condition, but the remaining code outside the parenthesis will be executed. Let us use a practical application of a 'while' loop:

```php
<? php
$books= 10;
while ($books > 0) {
echo "Selling a book... ";
$books - -;
echo "done. There are $books books left. < br / >";
}
echo "We are out of books!";
? >
```

The 'do while' loop

In the 'while loop,' we evaluate the expression at the start. However, when it comes to the 'do while' we do the opposite. We first run part of the code before we test the expression. Look at this example:

```php
<? php
$w = 1;
$l= 1;
do {
$w++;
$l++;
$area = $w * $l;
} while ($area < 1000);
```

> echo "The smallest square over 1000 sq. ft in area is $w ft. x $l ft.";
>
> ? >

In this example, the code inside the loop will run before the condition is tested. What this means is that the variable *$area* will at least have a value before we arrive at the testing phase. Now, if the area will continue to have a value of less than 1000, then the loop will continue to run.

The 'for' loop

So far you have learned about the while, and the 'do while' loop. But, there is one other type of loop that's more compact and neat, the 'for' loop. I would suggest that you use the 'for' loop when you have a specific number in your head which you want the loop to repeat. With the 'for' loop, you can create a counter variable which will record the number of loops. The syntax for a 'loop' is:

> *for (expression1; exression2; expression3) {*
>
> *// run the code*
>
> *}*
>
> *// Additional code goes here*

Looking at the above syntax, we realize that unlike the 'do while' loops which only have one expression in their parenthesis, the 'for loop' has three expressions. The expressions are described below in order:

- **Initializer**

This runs only once. The 'for' statement initializes a counter first.

- **Loop test**

This has the same function as the single expression in the 'do while' loop. So, if the expression test is true, then the loop continues, but if it is false, then the loop exits.

- **Counting**

This is used to change the value of the counter

The code snippet below is a demonstration of the 'for loop.' Kindly study it:

```
for ($1=1; $1<= 10; $1++) {

echo "I have reached: $1 <br />";

}

echo "finished";
```

This example shows how efficient a 'for loop' can be.

Loops and the break statement

When you are working with the 'do while' and many others, the loop will run until the point it is found to be false.

But, it is possible to exit a loop while it's in the middle by applying the 'break' statement. This operates the same way it does inside a switch construct.

Why should you break from this loop? Well, in some instances it is still right to exit out of the loop. For example, the infinite 'for' loop will continue to run and run until it exhausts the resources on the server.

Another reason why you might want to exit a loop is when you have completed doing whatever kind of process you wanted to achieve.

Creating nested loops

Have you ever heard of a loop within a loop? Below is an example of how a 'nested' loop will look:

```
for ($t = 0; $t < 10; $t++) {

for ($u = 0; $u < 10; $u++) {

echo $t. $u. "< br />";

  }
}
```

Strings

When it comes to programming, a string is a series of characters. For example, 'many,' 'how are you,' and 'morning' are all valid strings. In essence, the web is entirely made up of a string of data. HTML and XHTML comprise of strings. This part will take you through some of the crucial things you need to be aware of regarding strings in PHP.

Creating and accessing strings

To create a string variable is very simple, all it takes is to initialize your variable with a literal string value. For instance:

```
$yourstring= 'hello';
```

If you check the example above, the literal string is enclosed in single quotes. But, you can still use the double quotation marks. Something which you need to note is that both single and double quotation marks operate differently. A string enclosed with single quotation marks lets PHP use it exactly as it has been typed.

Here, the double quotation marks have several additional features:

- You can use special characters

- You can parse and replace

Create a string using this method

Earlier, I had taught you how you can create a string, but there are different other ways as shown in the examples below:

$yourstring= $mystring;

$yourstring = "how". "are". "you?";

$yourstring = ($x > 200)? "Bigger number": "Smaller number";

Length of a string

The function *strlen ()* will help you determine the length of a string. The function accepts the string value as the argument and outputs the length of the string. For example:

$yourstring= "goalpost";

echo strlen ($yourstring). "<br/>"; // outputs 8

Gaining access to string characters

Do you want to learn how you can access individual characters in a string?

PHP offers you with an easy approach. Study this example to learn:

$character = $string[index];

Arrays

At this point, you already know what a variable is in PHP. We said that a variable is a container which can hold a single value. However, there are specific types of variables which can store more than one value. An example of that variable is the array, and the other one is the object.

Arrays are an incredible feature in programming languages because it gives one the ability to work with huge sizes of data. As an excellent form of data storage, the two major properties of arrays are:

- An array has no fixed size, which means it can store millions of values

- It is very simple to manipulate multiple array values all at once

To begin with, let's first define an array.

Arrays are simply a unique form of a variable with added functionality. For example, arrays will help you store as many values in just one variable. Let's say, for example, you have a lot of soccer balls which you would like to store. If you want to store all your balls in a single variable, this is how your piece of code will look like:

$ball1= "Map";

$ball2=" Success";

$ball3 = "Mountains";

Assume, now that you have a list of books.

$book1= "Map";

$book2=" Success";

$book3 = "Mountains";

Well, suppose you wanted to loop through your list of books and pick one? Or let's assume that you don't have 3 books but 400? The best tactic to use here is the array. An array allows you to store all your books in one single variable name. Plus, you can access the array by using the array name.

In an array, each element stored has its own index to ensure that the process of accessing it becomes simple. PHP has three types of arrays, and we are going to discuss each type one by one.

Numeric array

This is an array that has a numeric index. A numeric array assigns each array element a numeric index.

To create a numeric array, you can use two methods:

- In this first example, the index is automatically assigned:

  $books = array ("Tom and Mary", "The happy ending", "The Storm");

- In this second example, the index is assigned manually:

  $books [0] = "Tom and Mary";

  $books [1] = "The happy ending";

  $books [2] = "The Storm";

Associative arrays

In this array, we will link the key with the value stored. But, when you want to store the type of data related to individual values, a numeric array is never the best to use. Instead, an associative array is the best option to go with.

This example uses an array to assign the age of various people:

  $ages = array ("David" =>22, "Peter" => 40, "Steve" =>37);

You can then use the ID keys in a script like:

  <? php

  $ages['David'] = "22"; $ages['Peter'] = "40"; $ages['Steve'] = "34"; echo "Peter is ". $ages['Peter']. " years old. ";?>

This code will display Peter is 40 years old.

Multidimensional arrays

When it comes to the multidimensional array, each element is an array. So, it is like we have an array of arrays. In the example below, we have created a multidimensional array with ID keys:

$class=array

(

"Geoffrey" =>array

(

"Meghan",

"Eden",

"Hazard"

),

"Jameson" =>array

(

"Mike"

),

"White" =>array

(

"Cleveland",

"Edwin",

"Junior"

)

);

This array would look this if written together with the output:

Array

(

[Geoffrey]=>Array

(

[0]=>Meghan

[1]=>Eden

[2]=>Hazard

)

[Jameson]=>Array

(

[0]=>Mike

)

[White]=>Array

(

[0]=>Cleveland

[1]=>Edwin

[2]=>Junior

)

)

If we want to display a single value from one of the arrays above, then we do that by using the following code:

echo "does". $class['Geoffrey'][2]. "belong to the Geoffrey class?";

This code will display the following: "does Eden belong to the Geoffrey class?"

Functions

A function is a block of code which performs a specific task. A function is defined by following a certain syntax, and then you can call the function from a different section of your code. The syntax that you should follow whenever you are creating a PHP function is:

function nameOfFunction ()

{

//Script to be executed

}

When creating PHP functions, one is always advised to give the function a name which corresponds to the task the function is going to do. The name of the function can even begin with an underscore or a letter, but it should start with a number. Here is an example of a function which will ask for my name:

<? php

Function Askname ()

{

echo "What is your name?"

}

echo "Please, ";

Askname ();

?>

The script will display the following: *"Please, what is your name?"*

Function parameters in PHP

If we want to increase the functionality of the function, then we need to add more parameters. You can look at a parameter as a variable. Parameters appear inside the function parenthesis. Look at the example below which uses parameters, the function is going to print several first names, but it will still retain the last names:

```php
<? php function showName($fname) {

echo $fname. " Rael. <br />";

}

echo "My name is ";

showName ("Kai Jam");

echo "My brother's name is ";

showName("Hoda");

echo "My cousin's name is ";

showName("Stuart") ;>
```

See the output below:

My name is Kai Jam Rael.
My brother's name is Hoda Rael.
My cousin's name is Stuart Rael.

In this example, the function *showName ()* has one parameter. It is still possible for a function to have more than one parameter.

Return values in PHP

If you want a function in PHP to return a value. We simply apply the 'return' statement. Consider this example:

```php
<? php function sum($x,$y) {

$total=$x+$y;

return $total;

}

echo "3 + 6 = ". sum (3,6);

?>
```

The output of this code will be 3 + 6 = 7

Chapter 3

PHP Form Handling

So far, you are now familiar with the basics of PHP and the way the PHP program works. You have also learned some of the core basics of the PHP language. I am sure you can declare a variable, write a PHP function, and many other important things which a person knowledgeable with PHP is supposed to know. From this point on, you will learn how to build practical PHP applications. One of the most popular capabilities of PHP is the ability to receive input entered by a visitor through an application. The previous scripts which we have done don't actually allow a user to enter values. However, if you can add that feature where a user can enter some values and read the input, then your PHP program becomes more interactive.

A common practice is letting the visitor of a web application enter some data is by using the HTML form. I know you have filled in a lot of HTML forms. Popular HTML forms include the contact form and order forms where you can order products from an online shop.

User input and PHP forms

The *$_POST* and *$_GET* are the two main methods used in PHP to get information from forms. The most important thing which you need to note down is that, whenever you are handling HTML forms together with PHP, all HTML form elements will also be present in your PHP code snippets.

This example has an HTML form and a submit button:

```
<html>
<body>
<form action=" home. Php" method=" post">
Your Name: <input type="text" name="firstname"/>
Your age: <input type="text" name="age"/>
<input type="Submit"/>
<form>
</body>
</html>
```

If the user submits the above form after entering the data, the form goes to the *home.php* file. The output of this form could be something like: "Welcome Mike! You are 30 years old."

Let's turn our attention to the PHP form validation. Whenever a user has entered data and clicked 'send,' it is important for the data to be validated by the client code. You can still perform browser validation. In fact, the browser validation is faster and reduces the server load.

However, if you are going to store your data in a database, it is recommended that you perform server validation. The best method to go with server validation is to post the form to the same page. Don't go to a different page. By doing this, you will help the user see the error message while they're in the same form.

$_GET is a built-in function which will help you collect values from a form using the method 'get.'

The Function $_GET

We use the built-in *$_GET* function to gather values from a form using the method GET. When you use the GET method, any information that is sent will be visible to everyone. The information will be displayed in the address bar of the browser. In addition, there are limits to the amount of information you can send.

So, when is it applicable to use the method get?

First, if you are fine with all of your variable names and values appearing in the URL, then you can use the method 'get.' But, you should never send your most sensitive data using this method. Again, large quantities of information are unfit for this method.

The $_POST Function

The *$_POST* function is another function which can be used in the PHP forms to collect values from a form after it has been sent from the method 'post.' The greatest thing with this method is that it provides security for your data. Nobody can see the information which you are sending. In addition, there is no restriction on the amount of data which you can send. However, an 8MB max size is the default size for the post, but still, you can change this on the *post_max_size* in your *php.in* file.

```
<form action="welcome.php" method="post">
Name: <input type="text" name="fname" />
Age: <input type="text" name="age" />
<input type="submit" />
</form>
```

When the data is submitted in the example above. This is how the URL will look:

"http://www.example.com/welcome.php"

The $_REQUEST Function

This function holds the details of the *$_POST, $_GET* as well as the *$_COOKIE*.

The *$_REQUEST* is a powerful function since it combines both the post and get. Before we can close this topic on form handling, it is also important to talk about the URL redirection. While it might not be related to the forms in a direct manner, URL redirection is something which you may have interacted with more than once. This is something you usually encounter when you fill out online forms.

Another helpful thing you can get by using the redirect feature is that you eliminate the possibility of users resubmitting the form when they reload the browser page. Instead, they refresh the page that they have been redirected to.

If you want to redirect your users to a given page, it will be very simple. No stress involved. All you need to do is write: *Location: HTTP header*, plus the URL you want to redirect.

The example below explains everything.

> *header ("Location: thankyou.html");*

Chapter 4

Introduction Databases and SQL

Making a decision about the way you store your data

As a developer, you need to note that when you start building applications which require you to store data, you must know which method your application will use to store the data. To help you make this decision. Here are some things that you should think of:

- The people who will access the data

- How much will the size be after, let's say, 10 years?

- What is the limit of my data?

- Will my application access the data frequently?

- The frequency of updates you may need to perform.

Once you have considered the above points, then you need to make a decision on which approach you are going to use.

A database management engine is the most popular model used when you want to store, modify, and retrieve data.

Database architectures

Before we can get started with the database topic, there are two options for database architecture which you can pick: a client-server and the embedded model.

An embedded database exists within the application which needs it. This means it runs on the same machine as the application host. In addition, it stores the data in the same host application machine.

Client-server models on, the other hand, these are flexible and powerful databases. Mostly, they are applied in networks. Database models come in two types:

- **Simple database model**

A simple type of database similar to an associative data array. Every data item is referenced using a single key. In this model, it is difficult to create a relationship between the data stored in the database.

- **Relational databases**

This gives one enormous ability and flexibility. It is among the most popular options. You will find that the relational database is common in the web sector. If you have ever heard someone mention RDBMS, then this is what they were referring to. Some examples of RDBMS in PHP include *PostgreSQL & MySQL*.

For this chapter, we will be focusing on the MySQL. The MySQL database model gives one of the following advantages:

- It is very popular across the web

- It is cheap and available in a majority of the web hosting accounts

- Very simple to use

- It is powerful, fast and can handle large complex data

- It is very easy to install, no complex steps to follow

- It can be installed for free

Relational databases in depth

As the name suggests, a relational database will offer the ability for data to be associated and categorized using certain attributes. For example, a record of students can be grouped by age, height, or date. In a relational database, data is organized in a table of rows and columns.

This is an example of a database table:

playerNumber	name	phoneNumber	datePlayed	nickname
42	David	555-1234	03/03/04	Dodge
6	Nic	555-3456	03/03/04	Obi-d
2	David	555-6543	03/03/04	Witblitz
14	Mark	555-1213	03/03/04	Greeny
2	David	555-6543	02/25/04	Witblitz
25	Pads	555-9101	02/25/04	Pads
6	Nic	555-3456	02/25/04	Obi-d
7	Nic	555-5678	02/25/04	Nicrot

In the table above, you should be able to identify the rows and columns. You will see that the rows hold information about every player while the columns are identified with a heading. This is called the column name or field name.

Normalization

In this table, you will notice that any time there is a match, all the details of a player have to be written down. It does not matter whether the details already exist or not. The end result is time wasting and repetition. Repetition of the same information such as the players' phone number is referred to as redundancy. Redundancy is unacceptable in a database. It wastes a lot of space and time.

Preventing redundancy is called 'normalization.' For instance, if we are to normalize the above table, we need to create another table for *playernumber*, *name*, *phonenumber,* and *nickname.* The table will look like this:

playerNumber	name	phoneNumber	nickname
42	David	555-1234	Dodge
6	Nic	555-3456	Obi-d
14	Mark	555-1213	Greeny
2	David	555-6543	Witblitz
25	Pads	555-9101	Pads
7	Nic	555-5678	Nicrot

You will now notice that on this table, each player only has one record. The player number is the unique field which identifies every player. Now that we have removed part of the players' information, we will create another table with the remaining details:

playerNumber	datePlayed
42	03/03/04
6	03/03/04
2	03/03/04
14	03/03/04
2	02/25/04
25	02/25/04
6	02/25/04
7	02/25/04

In this table, we have the *playerNumber* retained because it is the unique field which identifies each player. Now, if we can link up this second table and the previous one using the unique field, we can successfully associate a player and the date they played a match. In this example, we now say that the two tables are linked together using the *playerNumber* field. The *playerNumber* field in this last table is called the 'foreign key' because it points to the primary key in the previous table.

If you look at the above case, the only repeating information is the *playerNumber*. Therefore, we have saved a lot of space and time compared to the original table where we had to write all of the information. This type of relation is called 'one, too many' relations. This is because a single record of a player can be related to many other records if the player plays more than one game. The whole process that we have done is called normalization.

SQL

SQL is an acronym that stands for structured query language. SQL gives you the ability to carry out any operation related to the database such as creating a database and many other tasks. Even though this chapter focuses on MySQL, we will also mention SQL since it is another version

43

of MySQL. But, because the basics of SQL are similar to MySQL, then you can apply them to MySQL.

MySQL Data types

Any time you create a MySQL data type, you must specify the type and size of every field. The data types in MySQL include numeric, string, and date.

The numeric types of data

Numeric Data Type	Description	Allowed Range of Values
TINYINT	Very small integer	-128 to 127, or 0 to 255 if UNSIGNED
SMALLINT	Small integer	-32768 to 32767, or 0 to 65535 if UNSIGNED
MEDIUMINT	Medium-sized integer	-8388608 to 8388607, or 0 to 16777215 if UNSIGNED
INT	Normal-sized integer	-2147483648 to 2147483647, or 0 to 4294967295 if UNSIGNED
BIGINT	Large integer	-9223372036854775808 to 9223372036854775807, or 0 to 18446744073709551615 if UNSIGNED
FLOAT	Single-precision floating-point number	Smallest non-zero value: $\pm 1.176 \times 10^{-38}$; largest value: $\pm 3.403 \times 10^{38}$
DOUBLE	Double-precision floating-point number	Smallest non-zero value: $\pm 2.225 \times 10^{-308}$; largest value: $\pm 1.798 \times 10^{308}$
DECIMAL (precision, scale)	Fixed-point number	Same as DOUBLE, but fixed-point rather than floating-point. precision specifies the total number of allowed digits, whereas scale specifies how many digits sit to the right of the decimal point.
BIT	0 or 1	0 or 1

Date and time data types

Date/Time Data Type	Description	Allowed Range of Values
DATE	Date	1 Jan 1000 to 31 Dec 9999
DATETIME	Date and time	Midnight, 1 Jan 1000 to 23:59:59, 31 Dec 9999
TIMESTAMP	Timestamp	00:00:01, 1 Jan 1970 to 03:14:07, 9 Jan 2038, UTC (Universal Coordinated Time)
TIME	Time	–838:59:59 to 838:59:59
YEAR	Year	1901 to 2155

String data types

String Data Type	Description	Allowed Lengths
CHAR(n)	Fixed-length string of n characters	0–255 characters
VARCHAR(n)	Variable-length string of up to n characters	0–65535 characters
BINARY(n)	Fixed-length binary string of n bytes	0–255 bytes
VARBINARY(n)	Variable-length binary string of up to n bytes	0–65535 bytes
TINYTEXT	Small text field	0–255 characters
TEXT	Normal-sized text field	0–65535 characters
MEDIUMTEXT	Medium-sized text field	0–16777215 characters
LONGTEXT	Large text field	0–4294967295 characters
TINYBLOB	Small BLOB (Binary Large Object)	0–255 bytes
BLOB	Normal-sized BLOB	0–65535 bytes
MEDIUMBLOB	Medium-sized BLOB	0–16777215 bytes (16MB)
LONGBLOB	Large BLOB	0–4294967295 bytes (4GB)
ENUM	Enumeration	The field can contain one value from a predefined list of up to 65,535 values
SET	A set of values	The field can contain zero or more values from a predefined list of up to 64 values

SQL Statements

To succeed in working with databases and tables, you must learn and know how to apply SQL statements. Popular SQL statements include:

- SELECT

- UPDATE

- REPLACE

- INSERT

- DELETE

Other statements include:

- CREATE

- DROP

- ALTER

Connecting to MySQL using PHP

Well, now you are familiar with the MySQL database terms. We can now take you through a brief study of connecting your database with MYSQL. There are two ways which you can use PHP to connect to the MYSQL database:

- MySQLi (MYSQL improved)

- PDO (PHP Data Objects)

As you can see, the existence of the two methods points that each method has an advantage and a disadvantage. Which one is the best could just lead to an endless debate which we might never finish. In this book, we are going to use the MySQLi method.

The MySQL improved extension has the MySQLi class. To connect your database using PHP, follow the steps below:

1. You will require your MySQL server address. However, if the database exists on the same server, it will possibly be the local host.

2. Create a PHP file name, and you can name it as *connect.php.*

3. Type the PHP code below in your *connect.php* file. Make sure that you replace the username, password, and *dname* with your own details:

    <?php

    $mysqli= new mysqli ("localhost", "username", "password", "dname");

    ?>

4. Once the code has connected to the MYSQL, you can move on by selecting your database. You can also run SQL queries and do other operations that you want.

Retrieving data using 'select'

One of the most interesting things with the databases is the speed at which you can retrieve data in whatever order you want. Consider it as a database which stores books. If you want to display the contents of the database organized by the last and first name, SQL can help you achieve this quickly by using the ORDER BY statement:

"SELECT username, firstname, lastname FROM books ORDER BY firstname;"

47

Summarizing data

MySQL gives you the ability to summarize data instead of just presenting the actual data stored in the database. Use the following functions to summarize your data:

- *Sum()*

- *Avg()*

- *Max()*

- *Count ()*

Chapter 5

Manipulate MySQL Data With PHP

Inserting records

The SQL statement INSERT INTO helps one place records into a database table:

INSERT INTO name of table VALUES (v1, v2....);

If you only want to insert specific values, letting the remaining fields become nulls, you can use:

INSERT INTO name of table (field1, field2, ...) VALUES (v1, v2, ...);

To insert data into a table using PHP, first, we need to use the INSERT INTO statement and write the SQL query with the required values. The basic SQL INSERT INTO looks this way:

INSERT [INTO] name of the table (names of column) VALUES (values)

The square brackets around INTO are optional. It serves as a way to improve readability. The column names can be placed in any order. But, the values in the parenthesis must appear exactly as in the columns.

The picture below has a code snippet of how the INSERT INTO is used:

```
01.    <?php
02.    /* Attempt MySQL server connection. Assuming you are running MySQL
03.    server with default setting (user 'root' with no password) */
04.    $link = mysqli_connect("localhost", "root", "", "demo");
05.
06.    // Check connection
07.    if($link === false){
08.        die("ERROR: Could not connect. " . mysqli_connect_error());
09.    }
10.
11.    // Attempt insert query execution
12.    $sql = "INSERT INTO persons (first_name, last_name, email) VALUES ('Peter',
       'Parker', 'peterparker@mail.com')";
13.    if(mysqli_query($link, $sql)){
14.        echo "Records inserted successfully.";
15.    } else{
16.        echo "ERROR: Could not able to execute $sql. " . mysqli_error($link);
17.    }
18.
19.    // Close connection
20.    mysqli_close($link);
21.    ?>
```

We have to connect to the database first. Once the connection is done, the INSERT statement is executed. In this code, we are injecting data into a table of persons. The values we are inserting are the *fname, lname,* and email.

Once the records have been successfully inserted, a message will be displayed on the screen to inform us that the process has been successful. In case the process of inserting the records fails, an error message will be shown on the screen. Something else which you need to pay attention to is the way we have used the 'if, else' statement which we learned at the start of this book.

Insertion in multiple rows

SQL is a useful language which can allow you to perform the insertion of many rows into a database table by writing a single line of query.

In this example, we have added more rows to the table:

```
01.  <?php
02.  /* Attempt MySQL server connection. Assuming you are running MySQL
03.  server with default setting (user 'root' with no password) */
04.  $link = mysqli_connect("localhost", "root", "", "demo");
05.
06.  // Check connection
07.  if($link === false){
08.      die("ERROR: Could not connect. " . mysqli_connect_error());
09.  }
10.
11.  // Attempt insert query execution
12.  $sql = "INSERT INTO persons (first_name, last_name, email) VALUES
13.              ('John', 'Rambo', 'johnrambo@mail.com'),
14.              ('Clark', 'Kent', 'clarkkent@mail.com'),
15.              ('John', 'Carter', 'johncarter@mail.com'),
16.              ('Harry', 'Potter', 'harrypotter@mail.com')";
17.  if(mysqli_query($link, $sql)){
18.      echo "Records added successfully.";
19.  } else{
20.      echo "ERROR: Could not able to execute $sql. " . mysqli_error($link);
21.  }
22.
23.  // Close connection
24.  mysqli_close($link);
25.  ?>
```

Looking at the above example, you can see that every row is distinguished by a comma and surrounded with parenthesis.

Records update

The update statement is another useful statement which will let you make changes to the data stored in the table. We use the update statement together with the WHERE clause.

The basic form of an UPDATE statement looks like this:

"UPDATE table_name SET c1= value, c2 = value2, ...WHERE column_name=yourvalue"

Something you should always remember is that whenever you update a table, make sure you can tell the primary key. A practical approach to this is writing a query to the database and indicating all the records. After this, you can show these results together with a link to the update page.

But, for now, let's create a SQL query that has the UPDATE statement and the WHERE construct. After we have done this, we will move on to execute the query by passing the query to a *mysqli_query ()* function which completes the update function.

In our update statement, we want to update the table person's email address if the person in the 'person table' has an id of 1:

```php
<?php
/* Attempt MySQL server connection. Assuming you are running MySQL
server with default setting (user 'root' with no password) */
$link = mysqli_connect("localhost", "root", "", "demo");

// Check connection
if($link === false){
    die("ERROR: Could not connect. " . mysqli_connect_error());
}

// Attempt update query execution
$sql = "UPDATE persons SET email='peterparker_new@mail.com' WHERE id=1";
if(mysqli_query($link, $sql)){
    echo "Records were updated successfully.";
} else {
    echo "ERROR: Could not able to execute $sql. " . mysqli_error($link);
}

// Close connection
mysqli_close($link);
?>
```

As you can see, we establish a connection first with the database. Once the connection is successful, our UPDATE statement is the next to be executed.

Deleting a record

In the same way, you can update and insert records into a table. You can also delete the same values in the table with the help of the SQL statement. And don't forget that the DELETE statement is also used together with the WHERE construct to delete all records which fulfill a given condition. The DELETE construct is as follows:

DELETE FROM tble_name WHERE condition

However, something which you need to be careful with when using the DELETE command is that it is final. The moment a record is deleted, it will never be recovered. The record is gone forever. Don't confuse this with your computer where you have a recycle bin to go and restore your records. No! The action is permanent. The worst thing with this DELETE syntax is that the WHERE construct is optional. This means if you fail to put it in your code, every record is going to be deleted, and you will never recover it unless you have a backup. So, whenever you have to write the delete command, instead of the process being instant, you should display the records which you want to be deleted to the user to confirm everything first before you perform the deletion process.

Now, we can get into the practical side. In the picture below, the PHP code will delete the records of all those persons whose first name on the table is equivalent to John:

```php
01.  <?php
02.  /* Attempt MySQL server connection. Assuming you are running MySQL
03.  server with default setting (user 'root' with no password) */
04.  $link = mysqli_connect("localhost", "root", "", "demo");
05.
06.  // Check connection
07.  if($link === false){
08.      die("ERROR: Could not connect. " . mysqli_connect_error());
09.  }
10.
11.  // Attempt delete query execution
12.  $sql = "DELETE FROM persons WHERE first_name='John'";
13.  if(mysqli_query($link, $sql)){
14.      echo "Records were deleted successfully.";
15.  } else{
16.      echo "ERROR: Could not able to execute $sql. " . mysqli_error($link);
17.  }
18.
19.  // Close connection
20.  mysqli_close($link);
21.  ?>
```

Building a member registration application

In this section, I'll walk you through the steps of building a user registration application. The registration system will give users the ability to create an account by providing details such as their username, password, email and they can also sign out if needed. Also, you will learn how you can use PHP to restrict users from certain pages. In short, this practical application will make use of all the concepts we have learned in each of the chapters in this book.

First, let's set up our database

Now, I want you to create a database and assign it your favorite name. I will call my database 'registration.' As I said at the start, always try to give your variables, databases, and so forth, names which relate to the operation or function you want to do. Our registration database will have a table called 'users.' Our 'users table' has the following fields:

- Email

- Username

- Password

- User id

Below is the picture of my table:

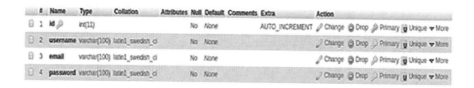

If you are not happy using the PHPMYADMIN wizard, you can go with the MySQL prompt. Just type the commands below:

```
CREATE TABLE `users` (
  `id` int(11) NOT NULL AUTO_INCREMENT PRIMARY KEY,
  `username` varchar(100) NOT NULL,
  `email` varchar(100) NOT NULL,
  `password` varchar(100) NOT NULL
) ENGINE=InnoDB DEFAULT CHARSET=latin1;
```

If you have successfully done that, then well done! You have successfully created a database. The next thing I would like you to do is to create a folder inside the root directory of your server. I want to assume that you are using WAMPP or XAMPP as your localhost. Locate the folder called *htcdocs* and create the folder inside it. Once you are done creating the registration folder, I want you to create the following files inside the registration folder:

- errors.php

- index.php

- login.php

- server.php

- style.css

If you have done that, open your files in your best editor. I am using Sublime Text 3.

User registration

```php
<?php include('server.php') ?>
<!DOCTYPE html>
<html>
<head>
  <title>Registration system PHP and MySQL</title>
  <link rel="stylesheet" type="text/css" href="style.css">
</head>
<body>
  <div class="header">
    <h2>Register</h2>
  </div>

  <form method="post" action="register.php">
    <?php include('errors.php'); ?>
    <div class="input-group">
      <label>Username</label>
      <input type="text" name="username" value="<?php echo $username; ?>">
    </div>
    <div class="input-group">
      <label>Email</label>
      <input type="email" name="email" value="<?php echo $email; ?>">
    </div>
    <div class="input-group">
      <label>Password</label>
      <input type="password" name="password_1">
    </div>
    <div class="input-group">
      <label>Confirm password</label>
      <input type="password" name="password_2">
    </div>
    <div class="input-group">
      <button type="submit" class="btn" name="reg_user">Register</button>
    </div>
    <p>
        Already a member? <a href="login.php">Sign in</a>
    </p>
  </form>
</body>
</html>
```

Go to the *register.php* file in your text editor. You can either copy and paste the code below or type it.

This picture shows an HTML form. But, some of the things which you need to note is the method 'action' which has been assigned to the *register.php*. What this one means is that when the user selects the register button, all the data contained in the form will go back to the same page. If you can still remember, when I was talking about the PHP form handling I did recommend that you apply this technique. At the top of this same page, I have included the *server.php* because some of this data is going to be received by the server.

You should also be able to recognize that we have included the *errors.php* file as a way to show errors from the form. Something else which you should see is that we are using the 'post' and not the 'get' method because we don't want anyone to see our information. Remember that we will be submitting data which has a password. Plus, the 'post' method works for data of just about any size.

Also, in the header section, we have put *CSS* links. There is a style sheet called *style.css*. I believe you already understand the role of *CSS*. So, open your *style.css* file and type the code below:

```css
* {
    margin: 0px;
    padding: 0px;
}
body {
    font-size: 120%;
    background: #F8F8FF;
}

.header {
    width: 30%;
    margin: 50px auto 0px;
    color: white;
    background: #5F9EA0;
    text-align: center;
    border: 1px solid #B0C4DE;
    border-bottom: none;
    border-radius: 10px 10px 0px 0px;
    padding: 20px;
}
```

57

```css
form, .content {
  width: 30%;
  margin: 0px auto;
  padding: 20px;
  border: 1px solid #B0C4DE;
  background: white;
  border-radius: 0px 0px 10px 10px;
}
.input-group {
  margin: 10px 0px 10px 0px;
}
.input-group label {
  display: block;
  text-align: left;
  margin: 3px;
}
.input-group input {
  height: 30px;
  width: 93%;
  padding: 5px 10px;
  font-size: 16px;
  border-radius: 5px;
  border: 1px solid gray;
}
```

```css
.btn {
    padding: 10px;
    font-size: 15px;
    color: white;
    background: #5F9EA0;
    border: none;
    border-radius: 5px;
}
.error {
    width: 92%;
    margin: 0px auto;
    padding: 10px;
    border: 1px solid #a94442;
    color: #a94442;
    background: #f2dede;
    border-radius: 5px;
    text-align: left;
}
.success {
    color: #3c763d;
    background: #dff0d8;
    border: 1px solid #3c763d;
    margin-bottom: 20px;
}
```

By using the *CSS*, the form will look very beautiful. Now, it is time to write the script which is going to collect the information submitted from the HTML form and store it in the database. This is going to be completed in the *server.php*. So, go and open the *server.php* then type in the following code:

```php
<?php
session_start();

// initializing variables
$username = "";
$email    = "";
$errors = array();

// connect to the database
$db = mysqli_connect('localhost', 'root', '', 'registration');

// REGISTER USER
if (isset($_POST['reg_user'])) {
  // receive all input values from the form
  $username = mysqli_real_escape_string($db, $_POST['username']);
  $email = mysqli_real_escape_string($db, $_POST['email']);
  $password_1 = mysqli_real_escape_string($db, $_POST['password_1']);
  $password_2 = mysqli_real_escape_string($db, $_POST['password_2']);

  // form validation: ensure that the form is correctly filled ...
  // by adding (array_push()) corresponding error unto $errors array
  if (empty($username)) { array_push($errors, "Username is required"); }
  if (empty($email)) { array_push($errors, "Email is required"); }
  if (empty($password_1)) { array_push($errors, "Password is required"); }
  if ($password_1 != $password_2) {
  array_push($errors, "The two passwords do not match");
  }

  // first check the database to make sure
  // a user does not already exist with the same username and/or email
  $user_check_query = "SELECT * FROM users WHERE username='$username' OR email='$email' LIMIT 1";
  $result = mysqli_query($db, $user_check_query);
  $user = mysqli_fetch_assoc($result);

  if ($user) { // if user exists
    if ($user['username'] === $username) {
     array_push($errors, "Username already exists");
   }

    if ($user['email'] === $email) {
     array_push($errors, "email already exists");
   }
  }

// Finally, register user if there are no errors in the form
if (count($errors) == 0) {
  $password = md5($password_1);//encrypt the password before saving in the database

  $query = "INSERT INTO users (username, email, password)
         VALUES('$username', '$email', '$password')";
  mysqli_query($db, $query);
  $_SESSION['username'] = $username;
  $_SESSION['success'] = "You are now logged in";
  header('location: index.php');
}
}

// ...
```

In this code, we are using sessions help track the users. A session is started by creating the *session_start()* at the top of the file. The comments in the code try to explain everything that is happening. However, there are a few things which I would like to talk about.

The 'if statement' helps determine whether or not the *reg_user* button located on the registration form has been clicked. Don't forget that if you go to our form, specifically on the submit button, the name attribute assigned to it is the *reg_user* which is the one being referenced to in the 'if statement.'

All data submitted from the form has to be analyzed to confirm that whatever the user entered was correct. Passwords have to be checked to ensure that they match. If the user keyed in every detail, then this means that there are no mistakes when the form is submitted. The details of the user will be successfully entered into the 'users' table. This way, the user registration would be successfully completed. Another important point to pay attention to is that the password entered into the 'users' table will be hashed. This means it will be secured so that no one can tamper with it. An advantage which comes with hashing your password is, if a hacker gains entry into your database, they will not manage to read your password.

In our current code, you can't see the error messages because we haven't written the *error.php* code. Well, if you want to display errors, type the following code into the *error.php* file:

```php
<?php if (count($errors) > 0) : ?>
  <div class="error">
    <?php foreach ($errors as $error) : ?>
      <p><?php echo $error ?></p>
    <?php endforeach ?>
  </div>
<?php endif ?>
```

In our registration page, we have created it in such a way that whenever a user successfully registers, the application will take them straight to the page called *index.php*.

Now, let's examine the user login. If there is something that's quite easy to build, it's the login page. Just open your text editor and type the code below:

```php
<?php include('server.php') ?>
<!DOCTYPE html>
<html>
<head>
    <title>Registration system PHP and MySQL</title>
    <link rel="stylesheet" type="text/css" href="style.css">
</head>
<body>
    <div class="header">
        <h2>Login</h2>
    </div>

    <form method="post" action="login.php">
        <?php include('errors.php'); ?>
        <div class="input-group">
            <label>Username</label>
            <input type="text" name="username" >
        </div>
        <div class="input-group">
            <label>Password</label>
            <input type="password" name="password">
        </div>
        <div class="input-group">
            <button type="submit" class="btn" name="login_user">Login</button>
        </div>
        <p>
            Not yet a member? <a href="register.php">Sign up</a>
        </p>
    </form>
</body>
</html>
```

Most of the things in this code resemble what was on the *register.php* page.

Now, when it comes to writing the code that will sign in the user, we have to do that in the *server.php*. So, open your *server.php* code and type this code at the end of the file:

```php
// LOGIN USER
if (isset($_POST['login_user'])) {
  $username = mysqli_real_escape_string($db, $_POST['username']);
  $password = mysqli_real_escape_string($db, $_POST['password']);

  if (empty($username)) {
    array_push($errors, "Username is required");
  }
  if (empty($password)) {
    array_push($errors, "Password is required");
  }

  if (count($errors) == 0) {
    $password = md5($password);
    $query = "SELECT * FROM users WHERE username='$username' AND password='$password'";
    $results = mysqli_query($db, $query);
    if (mysqli_num_rows($results) == 1) {
      $_SESSION['username'] = $username;
      $_SESSION['success'] = "You are now logged in";
      header('location: index.php');
    } else {
      array_push($errors, "Wrong username/password combination");
    }
  }
}
?>
```

Again, what this code does is that it checks whether or not the user has entered data in all the fields correctly and verify that all the credentials which were provided matched with the ones stored in the database. If they match the code, then it will log them in. Once the user is signed in already, they will be directed to the page where they will be told that they were logged in successfully.

Now, it is time to find out what is going on in the *index.php* file. Open the file and type in the following code:

63

```php
        <?php endif ?>

        <!-- logged in user information -->
        <?php if (isset($_SESSION['username'])) : ?>
            <p>Welcome <strong><?php echo $_SESSION['username']; ?></strong></p>
            <p> <a href="index.php?logout='1'" style="color: red;">logout</a> </p>
        <?php endif ?>
    </div>

    </body>
    </html>


<?php
    session_start();

    if (!isset($_SESSION['username'])) {
        $_SESSION['msg'] = "You must log in first";
        header('location: login.php');
    }
    if (isset($_GET['logout'])) {
        session_destroy();
        unset($_SESSION['username']);
        header("location: login.php");
    }
?>
<!DOCTYPE html>
<html>
<head>
    <title>Home</title>
    <link rel="stylesheet" type="text/css" href="style.css">
</head>
<body>

<div class="header">
<h2>Home Page</h2>
</div>
<div class="content">
        <!-- notification message -->
        <?php if (isset($_SESSION['success'])) : ?>
            <div class="error success" >
                <h3>
                <?php
                    echo $_SESSION['success'];
                    unset($_SESSION['success']);
                ?>
                </h3>
            </div>
```

In this code, we use the 'if clause statement' to check if the user signed in already. If they're not logged in yet, they will be taken to the login interface. This means that this page is only visible to users who are already logged in. Now, if you want to make certain pages accessible only to the users who have logged in, all it takes is to have this snippet of code appear at the top of the file.

In the second 'if' statement, we want to check if the user has already clicked the 'sign out' button. If it is evaluated as 'true,' the user is then logged out and taken back to the main page to log in. If you have done everything up to this point, then try to run your whole application. Attempt to register yourself as the new user. You can now personalize this site so that it suits your needs.

Chapter 6

PHP Sessions, Cookies, and Authentication

As you continue to build your web projects, there are complicated applications which will require you to monitor your visitors and users. You may not have built a login system, but you might need some certain details of your users. Some of these details could be the sessions of your users.

Different technologies have been created to help you accomplish this. Some of these technologies include browser cookies and HTTP authentication. These technologies will allow you to monitor your visitors through the use of a seamless process.

PHP Cookies

A cookie is a data object which a web server will store on your hard drive using the web browser. It can have any kind of alphanumeric information as long as it does not exceed 4KB, and it can be recovered from your computer and taken back to the server. Some of the popular uses of cookies include tracking session of users, storing the shipping cart, storing data from different visits, holding login details, and other functions.

Cookies are a private thing, this means, that not everyone can read them besides the website owner. This means that if a cookie is released by 'example.com,' it can only be recovered using the same domain. This is done as a way to secure the data and prevent external websites from having access to information which they are not allowed to have.

As a result of the internet's modern architecture, many websites can now release their own cookies. Cookies received from different domains are called third-party cookies. Third-party cookies are usually created by advertising firms as a way for them to collect information about a user as they visit different websites.

Since each website can have its own cookies, many browsers have an option to let users switch their cookies off both for the third-party and the server's domain. Luckily, when you turn off your cookies, you also turn off the third-party cookie for websites.

The exchange of a cookie takes place at the transfer of headers. This happens way before we send the HTML of a web page. The moment the HTML has been sent, it becomes difficult to send a cookie.

Well, learning how to send a cookie is not hard, the most important thing to know is that the HTML exchange should not take place before you have it sent. To define your cookie, you need to write the *setcookie* function. This function comes with the following basic syntax:

Setcookie (name, value, exptre, path, domain, secure, httponly);

If I want to create a cookie with a given name, and only want it to be visible across the web server's domain, this is how it will look:

Setcookie ('visitor', 'Job', time () + 60 *60*24*8, '/');

Accessing cookies

Reading the value of a cookie is not that hard. You can access a cookie by simply using the $_COOKIE array. For example, if you want to check if the current browser has a cookie with the name a visitor stored, we use the code below:

If(isset($_COOKIE['visitor'])) $visitor=$_COOKIE['visitor'];

Remember, you can read a cookie back after you have sent it to the web browser. In other words, if you release a cookie, you won't be able to read it until the browser refreshes the page or another website with access to your cookie happens to return the cookie to your server.

Destroying a cookie

So far you know how to create, access, and read a cookie. When it comes to destroying a cookie, you need to issue it once more and define a date. It is important that all the previous details of your cookie be the same except the timestamp. If they are not identical, you will not succeed in deleting the cookie. So, if you wanted to delete the cookie which we created previously, this is what you need to do:

setcookie('visitor', 'Job', time() - 2592000, '/');

Make sure that the time indicated should be outdated.

HTTP Authentication

The HTTP authentication also makes use of the web server as a means to control passwords and users of the system. This is appropriate for those web applications which require users to sign in.

For the HTTP authentication to be applicable, PHP has to transfer the header request which will then begin a dialog with the web browser. Now, for this feature to work, it must be on.

Username and password storage

MySQL is the popular method of storing data such as usernames and passwords. However, as you know, it is not a good thing to store your passwords in a manner in which anyone can easily access it. One of the ways we can avoid this is by using a method called a 'one-way function.'

This is a very easy function, and what it does is that it changes a string of text into a random string. The nature of these functions makes it very difficult for a hacker to reverse it. With the passing of time, we have come to see that the *md5* algorithm can be hacked, the same goes for the *sha1*. Which is why I recommend that you use the PHP hash function. To see how it works, we pass it a *ripemd* version algorithm:

$token = hash ('ripemd128', 'mypassword');

The end result of the token is a random string.

Salting

However, using hash on its own does not provide enough security for the database password because the chances are that if a hacker uses brute force, he will successfully retrieve the password. So, to solve this problem, we use a method called 'salting' before we finally apply the hashing. Salting is a process where we now add our own text to each parameter so that it can be encrypted. This is how it happens:

$token =hash ('ripemd128', '**mysaltstring**mypassword');

In the above example, the *mysaltstring* has been attached to the password.

Using sessions

You have already used this in the practical example. Sessions help you monitor what your visitors are doing when they move from one page to another.

Starting a session

To start any session, you must write or put the *session_start* function before the HTML, in the same way, that cookies are set. Now, if you want to save the session variables, you need to allocate them to the $_SESSION array by doing this:

69

$_SESSSION ['variable'] = $value;

If you want to read your session, you can do this:

$vartable =$_SESSION['vartable'];

Ending a session

The function *session_destroy*, will help you end or destroy a session.

Conclusion

Having read every chapter in this book, now you know how to write PHP code that can connect to the database, you understand the different database concepts, you can build a complete user registration system, and many more. Well, we also believe that you know how to write an innovative PHP code. Remember, PHP is an easy to understand language, and if you can give yourself sufficient time to practice, you will become a professional in PHP.

If you can master the basic fundamentals explained in this book, then you will be ready to start building PHP applications. PHP is an incredibly useful programming language which can help you develop robust applications. To become a great PHP developer, you have to put in a lot of effort. An excellent programmer should stay updated with the latest changes in the world of PHP to learn and understand the vital things that everyone has to know. Most importantly, I will suggest that once you have finished reading this book, the next step is to look for PHP books that have practical tests you can try. Get in-depth PHP books to help you understand the concepts better.

In this book, we have set the path for you continue exploring and learning deeper PHP concepts.

The next step you should take is writing your own PHP code. Practice every day until you master it.

Thank you and good luck!

PHP

A Comprehensive Intermediate Guide to Learn the Concept of PHP Programming

Introduction

Congratulations on purchasing *PHP : A Comprehensive Intermediate Guide To Learn The Concept of PHP Programming* and thank you for doing so.

Applications and dynamic websites are powered by a server-side scripting language called PHP. PHP is an acronym for Hypertext Pre-processor. Any server that has an installed PHP can run PHP scripts. Client computers that need to access PHP scripts must have only a web browser.

Since the introduction of PHP in 1994, the language has continued to drive the web industry. There are millions of websites which run on PHP, and that makes it a very popular language across the web. In truth, PHP is a red-hot property when it comes to creating websites.

A script is defined as a set of programming instructions interpreted at runtime. The language interprets scripts during execution and that gives it an edge. Usually, other software environments also embed scripts to boost the performance or execute routine tasks in an application.

Since PHP is being interpreted on the server, it is also considered a server-side script. An excellent client-side script example is JavaScript because the client browser interprets it.

By learning PHP, you acquire the best skills to help you set up your web application and perform different tasks. This book begins by introducing you to PHP and some of the powerful things that you can achieve with PHP. Later on, it goes deep into complex PHP topics like Restful APIs, PHP Graphics, and Object Oriented Programming. Additionally, it covers PHP Security and encryption and many other useful topics.

Chapter 1

All about PHP

What PHP Can Do?

PHP is a server-side scripting language. It is used all over the web and mentioned in most programming guides and web page tutorials.

In general, PHP adds a lot of functionality to websites created in HTML. But, how is that done? For those who know how to code in HTML, you might wonder how PHP relates to HTML, and how it can be integrated into a webpage. This chapter assumes that you are not a new beginner to PHP and you know how to run a PHP application. As such, only important parts of a code shall be explained because you already have a basic understanding of PHP.

You can consider PHP as a general purpose language even if the major reason for why it was designed is to generate web pages. Therefore, introducing PHP as a language that anyone can use to perform other functions besides the generation of web pages simply makes the task of learning the language difficult. That said; let's highlight some of the obvious functions that PHP does.

PHP Creates Web Pages

Practically, this means that the objective of a PHP program is to generate a JavaScript, HTML, and any other file found on the web page. In many cases, and especially when understanding PHP for the first time, the type of web technology that you will use is the HTML. As such, you need to know the type of web technology that a program runs.

Practically, this should not be a big problem since HTML is not difficult to learn and how PHP is integrated into HTML is fairly simple. Remember. Anyone can learn HTML because it is just a structural language. However, it is important to underline that you can find problems with understanding PHP programs because you may fail to comprehend the type of HTML it generates.

PHP as a Web Server

Knowing how the PHP Program selects the HTML needed to deliver to the web client is important. Usually, a request for a particular webpage by an internet user was sent to the web server. The web server looks for this file in the disk and once it finds the file, it sends it to the browser. Files are stored locally on the disk. Therefore, what the web server does is to select and send pages stored in the disk to the client web browser. This is not at all hard or complex.

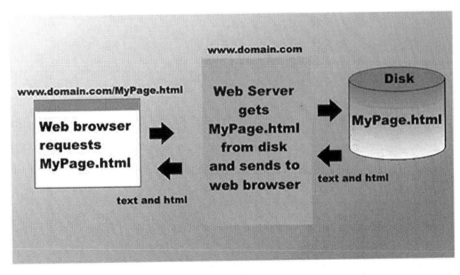

But remember that it is not the only way that a client can interact with a web page. If it is required that a webpage ending with an executable program should be produced by the web server such as mypage.exe, the web server will run the program on the server and gather the requested output and send it to the web browser.

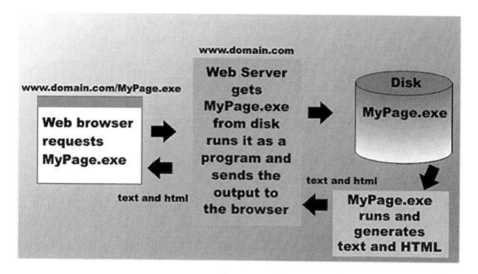

Obviously, the programmer is now allowed to create a program generating HTML and send the result to the browser without the user noticing any difference. This process is called Common Gateway Interface (CGI).

Currently, there are modern versions of CGI created to ensure that the entire process is efficient and powerful. In most instances, the main goal is to hide from the programmer whatever that is happening.

Languages used in web development such as PHP, ASP, and many others still have CGI even though the process is altered already. To go back to PHP, you must first write a PHP program. If a webpage is requested by a client, the server will load and run the program. The results are generated and then send to the client.

Remember, the server does not authenticate the output of the program. This means that even if the program generates an output that is irrelevant, the server will still transfer the output.

In addition, a PHP program runs on the server and not on the client machine. The program will transfer data to the client that is then portrayed as HTML. For that reason, PHP is considered as a server-side scripting language because of limited interaction with the client. Additionally, a majority of the processing takes place in the server.

Produce HTML

A PHP program contains a list of instructions executed procedurally. Take for example a simple PHP program that is similar to the popular "Hello world" program.

```php
<?php
  echo 'Hello';
  echo 'PHP' ;
  echo 'World';
?>
```

The instructions of the above program include three "echo" commands that select anything found in the quotes and send the results to the browser. See how a program begins with the <? php and ends with?>. Also, remember that a semicolon should end each PHP lines. An error message will be created if a semicolon is not included. Ensure that the Apache web server is started before running a PHP program. If you were to run the above short PHP snippet, you will see the following output:

HelloPHPWorld

There is a chance that you may doubt the idea that the PHP program produced only a plain text HTML without the markup tags as shown here. Well, that is still correct and if you use a different browser, it will display an unformatted text with a default font.

Notice also that the output of the program does not have spaces between the words. The reason for this is because the client browser receives exactly what you typed.

Direct Text

You have seen how the PHP echo command is used to send results to the browser. Still, you can send the output without using that command. For instance, if you add some texts outside the <? Php and? > tags, the output will still reach the browser without any changes.

This will allow you to include HTML blocks and a text that is found on the web page. Therefore, you can swap both text and PHP anytime that is needed. For example:

```
Greetings
<?php echo 'Hello';?>
--------------
<?php echo 'PHP' ;
  echo 'World';?>
```

This program will output the following line in the browser:

Greetings Hello...................................PHPWorld

Notice that the entire text shows up in a single line, although the PHP code didn't have the text in a single line. This is possible because a web browser ignores any line breaks found in the text that is sent to it. Most importantly, if you must have a line break, then you must place a <br/> tag in your code.

Installing PHP

You can use PHP in many different operating systems and platforms. Installing PHP in your machine gives you the advantage to create and test a web application on the go.

All in one package

There are very nice all-in-one Windows distributions that have PHP, Apache, MYSQL, and other applications in a single installation file like XAMPP or WampServer.

There is no problem that comes when you use these packages, although it is recommended to install Apache and PHP manually.

The PHP installer

While an installer can be found in the php.net, manual installation is advised when you have a running web server that is configured.

Manual installation

Installing PHP manually gives you several advantages:

- Back up and reinstallation can be done in a matter of seconds

- More freedom and control over Apache and PHP

Chapter 2

Restful APIs

In the modern era, different applications on different devices are connected with other application through APIS. Before starting to discuss REST API, let's define what an API is. You may already know what an API does or what it is, but still, there is no harm in repeating. This chapter assumes that you are new to API and for that reason, a basic intro about API is important.

In full, API stands for Application Programming Interface. The basic idea behind API is to link various applications regardless of their platforms to facilitate information sharing. Generally, API accepts requests from various applications, processes it, and sends back a feedback.

APIs allow you to perform the following functions.

• Create an API to allow third-party applications to communicate with your applications.

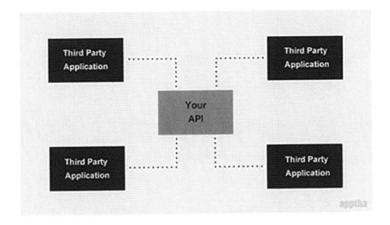

- Create your own API to link up with your own applications such as mobile app and websites.

- Make use of a third party API to connect and use their information.

What is REST API?

So far, you understand the full meaning of API. Let's now define REST API.

Representational State Transfer is the meaning of REST. This means that both the request and response must have some representation information. For instance, it should appear in a specific format. Basically, the requests should contain accurate HTTP methods and the response must be in the right format such as XML or JSON.

Think of REST API as a normal API that contains a set of principles. This implies that you need to follow a set of rules while building and consuming REST API.

Those rules include:

1. Use the correct HTTP methods while you make API calls. Below are the four major HTTP methods that one should use to send and receive API requests.

a. GET - To read multiple and single records

b. POST - To help create a new word

c. PUT - Used to update a record

d. DELETE - Used to delete a record

2. Use the correct URL hierarchy instead of a URL query string for API URLs.

   a. **Good URL**- http://example.com/api/products/1

   b. **Bad URL**- http://example.com/api/products.php?id=1

3. Don't use verbs as a resource name in the API URL and use nouns and proper HTTP methods instead.

   a. **Good**- http://example.com/api/products

   b. **Bad**- http://example.com/api/products/add

4. Make use of plurals for the resource names in the API URL

   a. **Good**- http://example.com/api/products

   b. **Bad -** http://example.com/api/product

5. Make use of HTTP response codes to show the status of the requests.

6. The response data should either be in XML format or JSON format.

The HTTP Client Libraries

HTTP stands for HyperText Transfer Protocol. This is the protocol that will allow you to send information repeatedly on the web. When you make an HTTP request, you will need to use the HTTP methods. That is POST, GET, DELETE or PUT.

Therefore, to use REST APIs, there must be a client with the ability to use HTTP methods. However, there is some limitation in this case such as it can only send GET and POST requests, and this is not enough to use REST APIs.

This means that you need to have an HTTP client library. And this is the time when CURL becomes important. CURL is the most popular and widely used HTTP client library among PHP programmers. This section will look at how to use CURL while consuming REST APIs.

Creating a REST API in PHP

Let's create a simple REST API in PHP using what you have learned so far. Assume that you have an online product catalog and you want your mobile application and website to share the same information about the products. This means that you are going to build an API that will allow you to add, read, update and delete products.

Assume your domain is example.com and example.com/api is the location of the API you are going to create. You will need to add a PHP file for the products to the folder /api/folder. The table below shows how the correct actions in the API are performed by the HTTP methods and URLs.

HTTP Method	URL	Action
GET	/api/products	Retrieves all products
GET	/api/products/5	Retrieves a single product of primary key 5
POST	/api/products	Adds a new product
PUT	/api/products/3	Updates a single product of primary key 3
DELETE	/api/products/7	Deletes a single product of primary key 7

The products.php file contains all the API code. In addition, you should remember that you will need to rewrite the URL so that it adheres to the rules of REST. Hence, add a .htaccess file to /api/folder and add the code shown below in it. This means that /api/products.php?product_id=5 becomes /api/products/5

```
RewriteEngine On # Turn on the rewriting engine
RewriteRule ^products/?$ products.php [NC,L]
RewriteRule ^products/([0-9]+)/?$
products.php?product_id=$1 [NC,L]
```

Rewriting a URL is a very wide topic that is not discussed here. If you are interested to learn about it, there are good resources online. Next, add the code shown below to help identify the HTTP request method.

```php
// Connect to database
    $connection=mysqli_connect('localhost','root','','rest_api');

    $request_method=$_SERVER["REQUEST_METHOD"];
    switch($request_method)
    {
        case 'GET':
            // Retrive Products
            if(!empty($_GET["product_id"]))
            {
                $product_id=intval($_GET["product_id"]);
                get_products($product_id);
            }
            else
            {
                get_products();
            }
            break;
        case 'POST':
            // Insert Product
            insert_product();
            break;
        case 'PUT':
            // Update Product
            $product_id=intval($_GET["product_id"]);
            update_product($product_id);
            break;
```

In this code, first, you have to connect to the database where you store the entire product's information. Next, use PHP super global variables $_SERVER to receive the HTTP request method applied in the API call.

To extract the products, use the get_products () function. In case you need to retrieve a single product, then you will have to pass this function to the product. If you don't pass the product ID, then this function will extract all the products.

```php
function get_products($product_id=0)
    {
        global $connection;
        $query="SELECT * FROM products";
        if($product_id != 0)
        {
            $query.=" WHERE id=".$product_id." LIMIT 1";
        }
        $response=array();
        $result=mysqli_query($connection, $query);
        while($row=mysqli_fetch_array($result))
        {
            $response[]=$row;
        }
        header('Content-Type: application/json');
        echo json_encode($response);
    }
```

To insert new items, use the insert product () function. Since the HTTP POST method is used to make API calls to insert products, the details of the new product are extracted from the $_POST variable itself.

```php
function insert_product()
    {
        global $connection;
        $product_name=$_POST["product_name"];
        $price=$_POST["price"];
        $quantity=$_POST["quantity"];
        $seller=$_POST["seller"];
        $query="INSERT INTO products SET product_name='{$product_name}',
         price={$price}, quantity={$quantity}, seller='{$seller}'";
        if(mysqli_query($connection, $query))
        {
            $response=array(
                'status' => 1,
                'status_message' =>'Product Added Successfully.'
            );
        }
        else
        {
            $response=array(
                'status' => 0,
                'status_message' =>'Product Addition Failed.'
            );
        }
        header('Content-Type: application/json');
        echo json_encode($response);
    }
```

To update a product, the update_product () function is used. Given that PHP doesn't have a $_PUT variable that is similar to $_GET and $_POST to retrieve values passed into it, you will have to use the input stream to fetch those values and update a product. You will learn how to pass values through an input stream while you use the API.

```
function update_product($product_id)
{
    global $connection;
    parse_str(file_get_contents("php://input"),$post_vars);
    $product_name=$post_vars["product_name"];
    $price=$post_vars["price"];
    $quantity=$post_vars["quantity"];
    $seller=$post_vars["seller"];
    $query="UPDATE products SET product_name='{$product_name}',
    price={$price}, quantity={$quantity}, seller='{$seller}' WHERE id=".$product_id;
    if(mysqli_query($connection, $query))
    {
        $response=array(
            'status' => 1,
            'status_message' =>'Product Updated Successfully.'
        );
    }
    else
    {
        $response=array(
            'status' => 0,
            'status_message' =>'Product Updation Failed.'
        );
    }
    header('Content-Type: application/json');
    echo json_encode($response);
}
```

If you want to delete a product, you will use the delete_product ()
function. First, select the product_id which you want to delete from the
$_GET variable.

```
function delete_product($product_id)
{
    global $connection;
    $query="DELETE FROM products WHERE id=".$product_id;
    if(mysqli_query($connection, $query))
    {
        $response=array(
            'status' => 1,
            'status_message' =>'Product Deleted Successfully.'
        );
    }
    else
    {
        $response=array(
            'status' => 0,
            'status_message' =>'Product Deletion Failed.'
        );
    }
    header('Content-Type: application/json');
    echo json_encode($response);
}
```

If you study all the above functions, you should realize that JSON has been used to format the output data. So, what you need to do is to combine all the code into one file called products. Php.

Consume REST API in PHP

Up to this point, you have learned how to create an API. The next thing you are going to learn is how to consume it. In this section, you will use CURL to consume the API.

There are built-in functions created for CURL in PHP. Below are some of the functions that you are going to interact with:

- Start a connection using curl_init ()

- Add request data using curl_setopt ()

- Send the request using curl_exec ()

- Close the connection using curl_close ()

The code shown below helps one select all the products. The API URL is passed to curl_init () function to help create a connection with the server and record the connection handle in $ch variable. In this variable, two options are defined using curl_setopt () function. The CURLOPT_HTTPGET method is used to indicate that the HTTP request method is GET and the CURLOPT_RETURNTRANSFER indicates that the response should return the value rather than display it directly.

Next, the request is sent through the curl_exec () function and the response is stored in a $response_json variable. Lastly, the connection is closed using the function curl_close (). Given that the response is a JSON string, you need to decode the string and convert it into a PHP array.

```php
$url = 'http://example.com/api/products';
$ch = curl_init($url);
curl_setopt($ch, CURLOPT_HTTPGET, true);
curl_setopt($ch, CURLOPT_RETURNTRANSFER, true);
$response_json = curl_exec($ch);
curl_close($ch);
$response=json_decode($response_json, true);
```

The next code is used to retrieve a single product and it resembles the code used to select all the products. In this code, the value 5 is passed to retrieve the product plus the primary key.

```php
$url = 'http://example.com/api/products/5';
$ch = curl_init($url);
curl_setopt($ch, CURLOPT_HTTPGET, true);
curl_setopt($ch, CURLOPT_RETURNTRANSFER, true);
$response_json = curl_exec($ch);
curl_close($ch);
$response=json_decode($response_json, true);
```

Next, you must know how to add a new product. This time, there are two CURL options. There is the CURLOPT_POST that indicates the HTTP request method. Both the POST and CURLOPT_POSTFIELDS are used to link the POST data.

```php
$data=array(
        'product_name' =>'Television',
        'price' => 1000,
        'quantity' => 10,
        'seller' =>'XYZ Traders'
);
$url = 'http://example.com/api/products';
$ch = curl_init($url);
curl_setopt($ch, CURLOPT_POST, true);
curl_setopt($ch, CURLOPT_POSTFIELDS, $data);
curl_setopt($ch, CURLOPT_RETURNTRANSFER, true);
$response_json = curl_exec($ch);
curl_close($ch);
$response=json_decode($response_json, true);
```

If you want to update a product, use the code below. In this code, CURLOPT_CUSTOMREQUEST is used to indicate that the HTTP request method is PUT. Given that there is no unique constant to link PUT data with the curl_setopt () function, you have to use CURLOPT_POSTFIELDS applied in POST request. However, this time, you don't pass the data as an array. But you will pass the data as a query string using the function http_build_query. This particular API will update the product using the primary key 3.

```php
$data=array(
        'product_name' =>'Laptop',
        'price' => 1200,
        'quantity' => 15,
        'seller' =>'ABC Trading Inc.'
);
$url = 'http://example.com/api/products/3';
$ch = curl_init($url);
curl_setopt($ch, CURLOPT_CUSTOMREQUEST, "PUT");
curl_setopt($ch, CURLOPT_POSTFIELDS, http_build_query($data));
curl_setopt($ch, CURLOPT_RETURNTRANSFER, true);
$response_json = curl_exec($ch);
curl_close($ch);
$response=json_decode($response_json, true);
```

To delete a product, you will use a CURLOPT_CUSTOMREQUEST to highlight the DELETE HTTP request method and this particular API call deletes the product that has the primary key 7.

```
$url = 'http://example.com/api/products/7';
$ch = curl_init($url);
curl_setopt($ch, CURLOPT_CUSTOMREQUEST, 'DELETE');
curl_setopt($ch, CURLOPT_RETURNTRANSFER, true);
$response_json = curl_exec($ch);
curl_close($ch);
$response=json_decode($response_json, true);
```

In conclusion, there is still a lot that you need to learn about REST APIs than what has been discussed in this chapter. The main focus of this chapter is to teach you the most important concepts on REST APIs. So far, you have a clear understanding of what REST API is, and you can now build it yourself.

Chapter 3

PHP and Internet Services

Before the discovery of HTTP, there used to be IMAP, POP3, FTP, and other kinds of protocols. A majority of people embraced the web browsers because it offered a cohesive program that could allow them to verify their emails, look at documents, and send files without any worry.

PHP has functions that support the use of these protocols. With the presence of these functions, frontend web applications that perform all kinds of tasks network-enabled can now be built using PHP.

Some of these tasks include sending a web-based email and searching for a domain name. Although it simplifies many of these tasks, it is good to identify the drawbacks and strength of each product.

Sending Emails in PHP

Situations arise where you are required to send an email message. Maybe you need to send a weekly newsletter to your readers or respond to a specific user action. So, how can you handle this kind of situation?

This section will take you through PHP mail and how you can use it to solve this problem. You will learn how to configure and use PHPMailer. PHPMailer is one of the most common mail sending libraries.

In general, email is a major part of any project, organization, and business. These days, being fast and responsive is very important, especially when serving your customers. Most of the time, responsiveness and well-organized communication are the main factor that users consider when making any purchase.

Although there are many ways that you can send emails, this chapter deals with PHP mail. There are two central ways to send emails through PHP.

1. Use the PHP in-built mail () function

2. Use a third party library like PHPMailer with SMTP

Let's now find out how each method works and how you can use it to send emails.

Requirements That You Must Have

Before you can start, make sure that you have the following things:

- A web hosting account

- PHP mail () function enabled

- An email account

- SMTP function enabled

- A domain that points to Hostinger MX records

Method 1: Use PHP Mail () function

The mail () function in PHP will allow you to send an email by using a local sendmail program. Any time you call the mail () function, it triggers a local sendmail program that is configured by the administrator. So, if you have your web hosted at Hostinger, you can enable and disable the function in Emails=>Mail Service Control part.

Usually, the sendmail service is, by default, enabled. However, if it is not, it is only a few clicks to make it active.

Step 1: Create a PHP mail test file

The first thing to do is to create a file for the PHP mail script. This file should be stored in public _html directory to ease the accessibility via the domain name. You can use the File Manager or even the FTP client for this particular task.

Step 2: Understand the PHP Mail

It is important to stay familiar with the components of a basic PHP mail script.

```php
<?php
    ini_set( 'display_errors', 1 );
    error_reporting( E_ALL );
    $from = "test@hostinger-tutorials.com";
    $to = "test@gmail.com";
    $subject = "Checking PHP mail";
    $message = "PHP mail works just fine";
    $headers = "From:" . $from;
    mail($to,$subject,$message, $headers);
    echo "The email message was sent.";
?>
```

The first two lines of the above code allow one to report an error. This will be important in case the script encounters a problem in the process of execution. The remaining components include:

- **$from** - Enter an email address that is created for your domain name to successfully execute the PHP mail.

- **$to**

- **$Subject** - Include the subject of your email address

- **$message** - This section contains the message of your email

- **$headers** - Help in specifying important information such as the sender address and reply-to location.

- **Mail -** the function which executes PHP mail

Step 3: Run the PHP mail script

If you have your PHP script stored in a public_html directory, then you can simply run it by accessing yourdomain.com/testmail.php. This is the last step in this particular method. Once you successfully run the test file, then you will be good to go with using the PHP mail function. Let's now turn to the second method.

Method 2: Use PHPMailer

PHPMailer is the most popular mail sending library used in PHP. This library supports sending an email through a mail () function or SMTP. In other words, PHPMailer is an efficient method that you can use to send emails in a PHP environment.

Step 1: Collect PHPMailer details

If you want to use PHPMailer with Hostinger SMTP, you should first set up an email account. You can achieve this by navigating to the Email Account section in the web hosting panel. Once you finish, gather your SMTP details found in the same section.

You should have the following four items:

1. An email account username

2. SMTP host

3. Password for the email account

4. SMTP port

Step 2: Installing PHPMailer

Once you have all the required details, you can start the PHPMailer setup process. One of the easiest ways to achieve this is by taking advantage of the Composer. If you are using a Hosting account, it is already preinstalled in the shared hosting plans, what you need to do is to connect it through SSH and run this command.

Cd public_html

Next, run:

composer require phpmailer/phpmailer

Wait for some time until the installation is over and PHPMailer will show up in a newly created vendor directory.

Step 3: Understand PHPMailer

Step 4: Run the PHPMailer script

In this step, you will create a testphmailer.php file and complete all the fields using the SMTP details. Run the script by typing, *yourdomain.com/testphmailer.php* in the browser and wait to see a message.

Step 5: PHPMailer contact form

The PHPMailer can also allow you to send complex messages. One way that you can achieve that is by creating a contact form that will allow visitors and users to get in touch with you. Below is an example of such a script.

```php
<?php
use PHPMailer\PHPMailer\PHPMailer;
require '../vendor/autoload.php';
    $mail = new PHPMailer;
    $mail->isSMTP();
    $mail->Host = 'mx1.hostinger.com';
    $mail->Port = 587;
    $mail->SMTPAuth = true;
    $mail->Username = 'test@hostinger-tutorials.com';
    $mail->Password = 'EMAIL_ACCOUNT_PASSWORD';
    $mail->setFrom('test@hostinger-tutorials.com', 'Mr. Drago');
    $mail->addAddress('example@gmail.com', 'Receiver Name');
    if ($mail->addReplyTo($_POST['email'], $_POST['name'])) {
        $mail->Subject = 'PHPMailer contact form';
        $mail->isHTML(false);
        $mail->Body = <<<EOT
Email: {$_POST['email']}
Name: {$_POST['name']}
Message: {$_POST['message']}
EOT;
        if (!$mail->send()) {
            $msg = 'Sorry, something went wrong. Please try again later.';
        } else {
            $msg = 'Message sent! Thanks for contacting us.';
        }
    } else {
        $msg = 'Invalid email address, message ignored.';
    }
?>
```

```
<!DOCTYPE html>
<html lang="en">
<head>
    <meta charset="UTF-8">
    <title>Contact form</title>
</head>
<body>
<h1>Let's get in touch!</h1>
<?php if (!empty($msg)) {
    echo "<h2>$msg</h2>";
} ?>
<form method="POST">

    <label for="name">Name:
    <input type="text" name="name" id="name">
    </label><br><br>
    <label for="email">Email:
     <input type="email" name="email" id="email">
     </label><br><br>
    <label for="message">Message:
    <textarea name="message" id="message" rows="8" cols="20">
    </textarea></label><br><br>
    <input type="submit" value="Send">
</form>
</body>
</html>
```

If the user submits his or her message, they will receive a confirmation message and the contents of the message will go to the e-mail box entered in the add Address field.

Tip

If the form created above does not work, then you can add this line of code to find out the problem:

$mail=>SMTPDebug = 2;

Once you solved the problem, set it to zero or delete it.

How to troubleshoot common PHP Mail and PHPMailer errors

It is very easy to master PHPMailer. However, errors can happen from time to time. The list below shows the most common errors that you may experience while sending PHP mail and how you can resolve it.

The sender address is rejected: it is not owned by the user

This error implies that the server is unable to validate the details presented. To resolve the error, navigate to the **from** headers to confirm that they correspond with an existing e-mail box. If that doesn't work, change it and the script will start to execute. Finally, confirm that your SPF record is enabled.

Gmail cannot verify that example.com sent this message

If you see this warning while testing a PHP mail script, it may mean the following:

- Your SPF record is disabled. Therefore, you need to enable it.

- The **from** header has an e-mail address which does not exist or owned by you.

Ensure that you have the correct SMTP authentication details.

Mail moves to a spam folder

There could be different reasons as to why a message may move into the spam box. Here are some of the common reasons:

- You have a wrong from headers.

- A spammy subject.

- The use of spam-trigger words

- The absence of an unsubscribe button from your mailing list. If more people report your emails as spammy, then your email will always move into the spam folder. That is the reason why you need to have an unsubscribe button so that users who aren't interested in receiving your emails can unsubscribe.

Reading Email with PHP

PHP has a great IMAP extension to help anyone use an email. However, to use this extension, you must install it and enable it before you can move forward.

Below is a PHP class that has some basic operations about an IMAP inbox. It is a bit customized to suit this particular project but still, you can change it to suit your needs.

```php
<?php

class Email_reader {

    // imap server connection
    public $conn;

    // inbox storage and inbox message count
    private $inbox;
    private $msg_cnt;

    // email login credentials
    private $server = 'yourserver.com';
    private $user   = 'email@yourserver.com';
    private $pass   = 'yourpassword';
    private $port   = 143; // adjust according to server settings

    // connect to the server and get the inbox emails
    function __construct() {
        $this->connect();
        $this->inbox();
    }

    // close the server connection
    function close() {
        $this->inbox = array();
        $this->msg_cnt = 0;

        imap_close($this->conn);
    }
```

```php
// open the server connection
// the imap_open function parameters will need to be changed for the particular server
// these are laid out to connect to a Dreamhost IMAP server
function connect() {
    $this->conn = imap_open('{'.$this->server.'/notls}', $this->user, $this->pass);
}

// move the message to a new folder
function move($msg_index, $folder='INBOX.Processed') {
    // move on server
    imap_mail_move($this->conn, $msg_index, $folder);
    imap_expunge($this->conn);

    // re-read the inbox
    $this->inbox();
}

// get a specific message (1 = first email, 2 = second email, etc.)
function get($msg_index=NULL) {
    if (count($this->inbox) <= 0) {
        return array();
    }
    elseif ( ! is_null($msg_index) && isset($this->inbox[$msg_index])) {
        return $this->inbox[$msg_index];
    }

    return $this->inbox[0];
}

    // read the inbox
    function inbox() {
        $this->msg_cnt = imap_num_msg($this->conn);

        $in = array();
        for($i = 1; $i <= $this->msg_cnt; $i++) {
            $in[] = array(
                'index'     => $i,
                'header'    => imap_headerinfo($this->conn, $i),
                'body'      => imap_body($this->conn, $i),
                'structure' => imap_fetchstructure($this->conn, $i)
            );
        }

        $this->inbox = $in;
    }

}

?>
```

A majority of this code is self-explanatory and has inline comments. However, it is good to explain the inbox () method because it is the main function. The IMAP inbox is just like an array that contains numbered key beginning from 1. In the inbox () method, it stores the index to enable email transfer, deletion, and reading.

Next, the header is placed in the function imap_headerinfo (). This selects an object from the server containing information such as Subject, From: address, To: address, and type of text encoding.

By using the function imap_body (), the text body of the email is extracted. What is extracted is just the raw body that has boundaries. In case the email received is in HTML, there will be a plain text and HTML version included. It is actually possible to parse via this data the same way an email client does, however, it is a bit messy.

Finally, to retrieve the structure, the function imap_fetchstructure () is used. This is important especially if you want to access email attachments.

So far, there is a lot that you have learned. We believe that you are familiar with PHP mail and you are able to use PHPMailer to send e-mails using SMTP authentication. Even though we have used basic examples to demonstrate the concept, the same syntax is applied when you want to develop a contact form and other extensions.

Chapter 4

PHP Graphics

GD Library

The GD library is important when you want to create dynamic images. The GD library is the best to use in PHP to create PNG, GIF, and JPG images quickly from the code. This will allow you to perform tasks like creating charts, build an anti-robot security image, and create images from different photos.

You can run the function phpinfo () to know if you have an installed GD library. It is downloadable online if you don't have one installed.

This chapter will cover the very basic of how you can create your first image in PHP. Since you have some PHP knowledge, it will be easy for you to interpret and understand the PHP codes.

A Rectangle with Text

```php
<?php
header ("Content-type: image/png");
$handle = ImageCreate (130, 50) or die ("Cannot Create image");
$bg_color = ImageColorAllocate ($handle, 255, 0, 0);
$txt_color = ImageColorAllocate ($handle, 0, 0, 0);
ImageString ($handle, 5, 5, 18, "PHP.About.com", $txt_color);
ImagePng ($handle);
?>
```

A PNG image is created by the code above. As can be seen in the first line, the type of content is assigned by the header. If you were creating a gif or jpg, then that would have changed accordingly.

106

The image handle is the next thing. ImageCreate () has two variables. Those two variables include the width and height of the rectangle. The rectangle dimensions of the rectangle created is 50 pixels high and 130 pixels wide.

The background color of the rectangle is set by the next line. The function ImageColorAllocate () is used to do that. Four parameters are accepted by this function. The handle is defined by the first parameter, while the rectangle's color is defined by the remaining three parameters. The color can be Red, Green, and Blue, respectively. The values that represent the color must be an integer in the range between 0 and 255. In this case, our rectangle is going to be red.

The next line of code after the background color describes the text color. There is no difference in format to the one used in selecting the background color. Our text color is black.

After the text color, the next thing is the text that you want to appear in the graphic. This is done using the function ImageString (). The first parameter of this function is the handle. It is followed by font, starting X ordinate, starting Y ordinate, the text, and finally the color of the text.

The final bit of this code is the ImagePng () function that creates the PNG image.

Play with Fonts

```php
<?php
header ("Content-type: image/png");
$handle = ImageCreate (130, 50) or die ("Cannot Create image");
$bg_color = ImageColorAllocate ($handle, 255, 0, 0);
$txt_color = ImageColorAllocate ($handle, 0, 0, 0);
ImageTTFText ($handle, 20, 15, 30, 40, $txt_color, "/Fonts/Quel.ttf", "Quel");
ImagePng ($handle);
?>
```

This code resembles the previous code except that there is the ImageTTFText() function instead of the ImageString ().

The first parameter is the handle, and then followed by the font size, rotation, starting X, starting Y, text color, font, and then the text. When it comes to the font parameter, it is important to show the path to the font line. For instance, if you look at the code above, the font Quel is located in a folder named Fonts. So, if your text doesn't show up, then the path that leads to your font is wrong. Another reason is that maybe your text is positioned outside the viewable area by the Y and X rotational parameters.

Drawing lines

```php
<?php header ("Content-type: image/png");
$handle = ImageCreate (130, 50) or die ("Cannot Create image");
$bg_color = ImageColorAllocate ($handle, 255, 0, 0);
$txt_color = ImageColorAllocate ($handle, 255, 255, 255);
$line_color = ImageColorAllocate ($handle, 0, 0, 0);
ImageLine($handle, 65, 0, 130, 50, $line_color);
ImageString ($handle, 5, 5, 18, "PHP.About.com", $txt_color);
ImagePng ($handle);
?>
```

The code uses the ImageLine () function in drawing a line. The first parameter is the handle that is followed by the starting X and Y, the closing X and Y, and finally, the color. If you would like to create a volcano, then you need to include the code below into a loop. Make sure you maintain the coordinates but move along the x-axis with the finishing coordinates.

```php
<?php
header ("Content-type: image/png");
$handle = ImageCreate (130, 50) or die ("Cannot Create image");
$bg_color = ImageColorAllocate ($handle, 255, 0, 0);
$txt_color = ImageColorAllocate ($handle, 255, 255, 255);
$line_color = ImageColorAllocate ($handle, 0, 0, 0);
for($i=0;$i<=129;$i=$i+5)
{
ImageLine($handle, 65, 0, $i, 50, $line_color);
}
ImageString ($handle, 5, 5, 18, "PHP.About.com", $txt_color);
ImagePng ($handle);
?>
```

Arcs and Pies

```php
<?
header('Content-type: image/png');
$handle = imagecreate(100, 100);
$background = imagecolorallocate($handle, 255, 255, 255);
$red = imagecolorallocate($handle, 255, 0, 0);
$green = imagecolorallocate($handle, 0, 255, 0);
$blue = imagecolorallocate($handle, 0, 0, 255);
imagefilledarc($handle, 50, 50, 100, 50, 0, 90, $red, IMG_ARC_PIE);
imagefilledarc($handle, 50, 50, 100, 50, 90, 225 , $blue, IMG_ARC_PIE);
imagefilledarc($handle, 50, 50, 100, 50, 225, 360 , $green, IMG_ARC_PIE);
imagepng($handle);
?>
```

By using the imagefilledarc, you can develop a pie. The parameters consist of the handle, height, color, type, width, and center X & Y. Some examples of types include:

1. IMG_ARC_PIE-Filled arch

2. IMG_ARC_CHORD-has a straight edge

3. IMG_ARC_NOFIL

4. IMG_ARC_EDGED-Connects to the center. Use it together with the unfilled pie.

It is possible to lay a second arc such that it creates a 3D effect. To achieve this, add the code below to the first filled arc.

```php
$darkred = imagecolorallocate($handle, 0x90, 0x00, 0x00);
$darkblue = imagecolorallocate($handle, 0, 0, 150);
// 3D look for ($i = 60; $i > 50; $i--) {
 imagefilledarc($handle, 50, $i, 100, 50, 0, 90, $darkred,
  IMG_ARC_PIE); imagefilledarc($handle, 50, $i, 100, 50, 90, 360 ,
   $darkblue, IMG_ARC_PIE);
   }
```

Finalize the Basics

```php
<?php
header ("Content-type: image/gif");
$handle = ImageCreate (130, 50) or die ("Cannot Create image");
$bg_color = ImageColorAllocate ($handle, 255, 0, 0);
$txt_color = ImageColorAllocate ($handle, 0, 0, 0);
ImageString ($handle, 5, 5, 18, "PHP.About.com", $txt_color);
ImageGif ($handle);
?>
```

So far, you have only learned how to create PNG image formats. The code snippet shown above creates a GIF using the ImageGif () function.

Why You Should Use PHP for Web Graphics

PHP is the most popular and powerful dynamic programming language applied in web development and general purposes. It is a language of the server that allows anyone to perform multiple functions in a website that can't be achieved using a scripting language such as HTML. The ability to connect it to the MySQL database makes it the best scripting language. It is fast because it doesn't require heavy coding.

Web pages are made responsive by using PHP. Graphics are one of the best features of PHP. It has powerful GD graphics library that can dynamically change images. Furthermore, it can create PNG, JPEGs, GIFs, and WBMPs.

By using GD graphics library, it adds another advantage to PHP. Bar diagrams, Charts, graphs, and line diagrams can be created easily with dynamic properties. Building a graphical data chart is very easy when you use this language.

PHP will allow anyone to create image objects such as rectangle, circle, oval, and others which can be altered to create complex patterns and designs. PHP facilitates grouping of large, complex objects as well as the representation of dynamic properties to image objects.

The graphics library supports a variation of Z-index. Z-index refers to the ability to alter objects above or behind other objects. When it comes to web development, this property is very important in adding dynamic visual properties. It involves the production of multiple layers in a website where objects are organized.

Scaling an image is an important factor required in websites. While people browse the internet from different devices such as cellphones and iPad, the display of websites is expected to be responsive. This means that a website has to fit the size of a browser without losing any of its property. And a PHP script is the best to achieve this function.

Chapter 5

Classes and Objects

In this chapter, you will learn about PHP classes and objects. You will be introduced to the most important concepts in PHP Object Oriented programming.

Object-oriented programming takes a different approach. Here, problems are modeled and processed using objects. As a result, an object-oriented application has similar objects and collaborates with other objects to offer a solution to a problem.

The key building blocks of object-oriented programming include classes and objects. Problems are modeled and processed with the help of objects. Therefore, having knowledge about objects and classes and the difference between the two is very crucial.

PHP Objects and Classes

In reality, objects have its own characteristics and behavior. You can group similar objects that share the same characteristics and behaviors into a single class. So you can consider an object as an instance of the class.

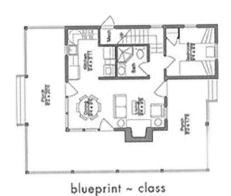

blueprint ~ class   houses ~ objects

Definition of Classes and Objects

Before you can move on and create a new object, you need to have a blueprint of the object or even a class. It is not hard to define a new class in PHP. The only thing you need to do is to use the class keyword as shown below:

```php
<?php
class BankAccount{

}
```

The example above defines a new empty class called BankAccount. Now, by using the BankAccount class, it is possible to create a new bank account object that uses the new keyword as shown below:

```php
<?php
class BankAccount{

}

// create a new bank account object
$account = new BankAccount();

var_dump($account);
```

You should see that var_dump () function is used to view the content of the bank account.

Properties

When it comes to object-oriented, the characteristics of an object are referred to as properties. For instance, if you use the bank account example, a bank account has an account number and total balance. Now, you can use those two properties to add to the BankAccount class.

```php
<?php
class BankAccount{
  private $accountNumber;
  private $totalBalance;
}
```

You should notice something special in this code. The keyword private is used before the properties. This is referred to as property visibility. Each property can have either one of the three property visibility. That includes private, public, and protected.

Private

If the properties of a class are considered private, it means that they are only accessible by the methods found inside the class. Later on, you will learn more about the methods of a class.

114

Protected

When the properties of a class are protected, they can only be accessible by the subclasses. You will also learn about subclasses and inheritance later.

Public

Lastly, if the properties of a class are public, this means that they can only be accessed by the methods inside and the code that is outside the class.

So, going back to the BankAccount class example, you can only access the properties of the bank account while inside the class because they are protected.

Methods

So far, you have some basic knowledge of classes, objects, and its properties. How about methods? Methods are also an important element in object-oriented programming. The behaviors of the object or class are referred to as methods. This is similar to class properties. Methods can also have three different levels of visibility. A method can be private, protected, and public.

Transactions that can take place in a bank account include the deposit of money, cash withdrawal, and balance check. Also, you need methods to help you set the bank account number as well as select the bank account number. The bank account number is important in differentiating one bank account to the other.

When you want to create a method for a class, the function keyword should precede the name and parentheses. A method resembles a function in PHP with the only difference being that a method is related to a class and has the property visibility level. Similar to normal PHP functions, a method can have one or more parameter and can return a value. Now that you have learned about methods, let's add some methods to our BankAccount class.

```php
<?php
class BankAccount{
/**
 * bank account number
 * @var string bank account number
 */
private $accountNumber;
/**
 * total balance
 * @var float total balance
 */
private $totalBalance;

/**
 * deposit money to the bank account
 * @param float $amount amount to deposit
 */
public function deposit($amount){
$this->totalBalance += $amount;
}

/**
 * withdraw money from the bank account
 * @param double $amount
 */
public function withdraw($amount){
if($amount > $this->totalBalance)
die('Not enough money to withdraw');

$this->totalBalance -= $amount;
}
```

```php
/**
 * returns total balance
 * @return float total balance
 */
public function getBalance(){
return $this->totalBalance;
}

/**
 * return bacnk account number
 */
public function getAccountNumber(){
return $this->accountNumber;
}

/**
 * set bank account number
 * @param string $accountNumber
 */
public function setAccountNumber($accountNumber){
$this->accountNumber = $accountNumber;

}
}
```

You should notice that in this code, there is a unique $this variable applied to help access property of an object. In PHP, the $this variable is used to point to the current object.

If you want to access a property, use the arrow (=>) operator as shown below.

    object->property

Bank Account's Methods in Deep

- The method deposit () increases the total balance of the account.

- The method withdraw () determines the available balance. In case the total balance is less than the amount to withdraw, an error message is sent.

- The method setAccountNumber () and getAccountNumber () are referred to as setter-getter methods.

- The method getBalance () displays the total balance of the account.

Calling methods

To call a method of an object, use this => operator followed by the method's name and parentheses. This example demonstrates how you can call the methods of the bank account class:

```
// create a new bank account object
$account = new BankAccount();

$account->setAccountNumber('1243845355');
echo sprintf("Bank account # %s<br/>",$account->getAccountNumber());

echo sprintf("Deposit $2000 to the bank account.<br/>");
$account->deposit(2000);
echo sprintf("Total balance %0.2f<br/>", $account->getBalance());

echo sprintf("Withdraw $100 from the bank account.<br/>");
$account->withdraw(100);
echo sprintf("Total balance %0.2f<br/>", $account->getBalance());

echo sprintf("Withdraw $2000 from the bank account.<br/>");
$account->withdraw(2000);
```

The basics of OOP have been learned in this chapter. You have briefly learned how you can define a class in PHP, an instantiated object with the name of a class, and methods. This is just but an introduction, there is a lot more to classes and objects than this simple introduction. This chapter has focused only on the very basic concepts. Hopeful, in the later chapter, you will learn more on OOP in PHP.

118

Chapter 6

Security and Encryption

One of the best features of PHP is its level of flexibility. This language was designed to process forms in HTML pages, and thus, PHP eases the process of sending form data. Convenience is an upper hand in programming. However, the same features that can help you achieve various tasks in PHP can still be an avenue for those who want to hack into your system.

It is important to recognize that PHP, on its own, is neither secure nor unsecure. The security of your web application is defined by the type of code that you write. Consider a PHP script that opens a file that contains a name that was passed in a form parameter. If you fail to check the filename, there is a chance that a user can reveal a URL, the name of the path or even a path to exit from the application data directory and get into a system directory.

Web security is an evolving field. So, this chapter alone cannot sufficiently teach you how you can prevent attacks directed into your application. This chapter simply covers a few important topics related to security. Furthermore, you will learn some tips on how you can protect your applications from dangerous attacks.

Filter Input

One of the most critical things to be aware of when building a secure application is that any information not produced inside the application is vulnerable to infection. This means that the data can be infected or malicious.

When data is infected or tainted, it doesn't mean that it is already malicious. It only means that you don't trust the security of the source. For this reason, you need to assess it to make sure that it is free from infection. This process of assessing data to ensure that it is authentic before it enters your application is called filtering. Below are some few practices related to the filtering process.

- Don't try to fix the wrong data. Trying to correct invalid data always results in security vulnerabilities.

- Apply the whitelist approach. This approach requires one to assume that data is invalid.

- Use a naming procedure to distinguish filtered and tainted data.

Don't forget that the objective of filtering is to prove whether the data is valid or not.

Let's consider a simple HTML form that can allow users to choose between three colors:

```
<form action = "process.php" method = "POST"
Choose a color:
<select name="color">
<option value = "red">red</option>
<option value = "green">green</option>
<option value = "blue">blue</option>
</select>
<input type ="submit"/>
</form>
```

It is very easy to embrace the $_POST ['color'] in process.php. After all, this form dictates the user what he or she can enter. But experienced developers are aware that an HTTP request is not necessarily sent by a browser being used by a genuine user. There are different ways in which malicious data can find a way into your application. So, the only way to remain secure is to filter all your input.

SQL Injection

This is the second most popular web vulnerability. It is similar to XSS. However, the difference is that an SQL injection happens when un-escaped data exists in an SQL query. SQL injection vulnerability affects web applications that have an SQL database.

This is very dangerous because attackers take advantage of the SQL injection vulnerability to by-pass a web application and steal contents of a whole database. Furthermore, SQL injections can modify, delete, and add records in a database. And this can impact the integrity of the whole data. As you can see, SQL injections are very risky because attackers use it to gain entry into a database.

How It Works

To successfully run malicious SQL queries against a database server, an attacker has to identify an input in the web application that is written in the SQL query.

Then, for the attack to be possible, the vulnerable website has to store the details of the user in the SQL statement. This allows the attacker to insert a payload that will combine with the SQL query and run against the database server. Below is a server script that validates users into a web application.

```
# Define POST variables
uname = request.POST['username']
passwd = request.POST['password']

# SQL query vulnerable to SQLi
sql = "SELECT id FROM users WHERE username='" + uname +
"' AND password='" + passwd + "'"

# Execute the SQL statement
database.execute(sql)
```

This is a simple example to demonstrate how one can validate users against a database table. However, SQL injections can still attack this script since a harmful input can be submitted by an attacker which will affect the SQL statement processed in the database server.

An attacker can also direct how the entire SQL query should run by commenting on the entire SQL statement.

Once the query has finished executing, the result returns to the application for further processing. The end result is an authentication bypass that will log in the attacker as an administrator.

What is the worst that an attacker can perform with an SQL?

The SQL language is used to delete, add, edit, and access data in an RDMS. Besides that, there are instances when an RDBMS can execute commands in the operating system from an SQL statement. By considering this, you will start to understand the significance of a successful SQL injection attack.

- An attacker can apply an SQL injection to impersonate users.

- Because of the vulnerability of an SQL injection, it can reveal the whole data stored in a database.

- The database's entire data can also be deleted by an attacker using SQL.

Anatomy of SQL Injection Attack

Two conditions are also needed to exist for an SQL injection. That includes:

1. A user controllable input that is applied directly into an SQL query.

2. An RDMS that has an SQL.

The example above assumes that the goal of the attacker is to infect data in a database by manipulating the vulnerability of an SQL injection.

Creating an SQL statement by using the wrong input may cause a database server to send an error. It is not bad to experience errors while developing an application. However, if the error is allowed to show up on the user's side, it might reveal additional information about the structure of the system to the hacker. For that reason, it is advised to hide errors from users because SQL errors are very descriptive to disclose the organization of the database.

Escape Output

The importance of filtering all the input data is learned at the beginning of this chapter. Besides that, it is possible that even though the data is filtered, it still has characters that have a special feature based on the medium in which your application wants to display it. That channel can be SQL, HTML or XML. For that reason, it is important to escape output.

You know that output refers to any data which leaves an application and goes to the next application or client. The receiving application expects data to be of a given format such as SQL and HTML. Additionally, this format might consist of characters and any other information that has an exceptional significance to the receiving application or client.

Escaping is sometimes called encoding. In other words, it is the process where you represent data in a manner that is not interpreted. For example, HTML will display the text below in a Web browser as bold-faced as a result of the <strong> tags.

    <strong>This is bold text</strong>

However, if you need to display the tags in the browser and prevent their interpretation, then you will require escaping the angle brackets. Remember, the angle brackets have a unique meaning in HTML. Below is an example of an escaped HTML.

<strong>This is bold text.</strong>

Escaping output is not a hard process. At least, it might need the addition of several lines of code or paying attention to detail. The most important thing to remember is the formatted output and the unique characters that must be escaped in the format.

Cross-Site Scripting

Cross-site scripting (XSS) is another common web security vulnerability.

Generally, vulnerability exists anytime you display un-escaped data. For instance:

```
<? Php

    Echo $_POST['username'];

?>
```

Based on history, XSS has been used to record the cookies of a victim. To prevent XSS, the input must be escaped out.

More Tips on Security

Since security is an important concept, pay attention to the following points.

- Make sure to filter all input data you get from remote sources. Employ a strict filtering logic.

- Escape the output to ensure that data is not misinterpreted by a remote system.

- Disable the register_globals and allow_url_fopen.

- Anytime you construct a filename, review the components using realpath () and baseaname ().

124

- Make it a habit to call session_regenerate_id() any time the privilege level of a user changes.

- Avoid using data supplied from a user using eval (), preg_replace (), and any system commands.

Chapter 7

Regular Expressions

In the following chapter, you will learn about regular expressions in PHP and how a programmer can apply them in pattern matching.

Regular Expression-Definition

They are popularly referred to as "regex" or "RegExp". Usually, they are uniquely formatted text strings that one can use to determine patterns in a text. Regular expressions are very useful when it comes to processing a text and manipulating a text. For instance, an individual can use it to determine if the data format such as name, phone number, and email typed by the user is correct or not, find or replace a matching string in text content, and many others.

Starting from PHP version 5.3 and above, it allows Perl style regular expressions through preg_family of functions. So, why Perl style regular expressions? Well, the answer is because Perl is a leading mainstream programming language that offers an integrated support for regular expression. In addition, it is popular because it supports regular expressions and has extraordinary text processing and manipulation ability.

The table below shows some of the most common PHP in-built pattern matching functions.

Function	What it Does
preg_match()	Perform a regular expression match.
preg_match_all	Perform a global regular expression match.
preg_replace()	Perform a regular expression search and replace.
preg_grep()	Returns the elements of the input array that matched the pattern.
preg_split()	Splits up a string into substrings using a regular expression.
preg_quote()	Quote regular expression characters found within a string.

Tip

The PHP preg_match () function will stop to search once it finds the first match. On the other hand, the preg_match_all () function will continue to search until it reaches the end of the string and identifies all the possible matches instead of halting at the first match.

The Syntax of A Regular Expression

The syntax of a regular expression has special characters. The specific type of characters that have a unique meaning inside a regular expression include: . * ? + [ ] ( ) { } ^ $ | \.

However, before you can use these characters, you must backslash them. For instance, if you want to match ".", you will need to write \. Other remaining characters assume their literal meaning automatically.

The sections below describe several available options for formulating patterns:

Character classes

The square brackets which enclose a pattern of characters are referred to as a character class. A character class will match a single character from a list of unique characters.

Negated character classes can also be generated that match any type of character except the ones that are inside the brackets. To define a negated character class, the caret symbol should immediately follow the opening bracket. Example, [^abc].

Still, it is possible to define a range of characters by placing the hyphen (-) character inside a character such as [0-9]. Below are examples of character classes.

RegExp	What it Does
[abc]	Matches any one of the characters a, b, or c.
[^abc]	Matches any one character other than a, b, or c.
[a-z]	Matches any one character from lowercase a to lowercase z.
[A-Z]	Matches any one character from uppercase a to uppercase z.
[a-Z]	Matches any one character from lowercase a to uppercase Z.
[0-9]	Matches a single digit between 0 and 9.
[a-z0-9]	Matches a single character between a and z or between 0 and 9.

The example below demonstrates how to determine whether a pattern is present in a string or not by using regular expressions and the PHP preg_match () function.

```php
<?php
$pattern = "/ca[kf]e/";
$text = "He was eating cake in the cafe.";
if(preg_match($pattern, $text)){
    echo "Match found!";
} else{
    echo "Match not found.";
}
?>
```

At the same time, all matches in a string can be identified by applying the the preg_match_all () function:

```php
<?php
$pattern = "/ca[kf]e/";
$text = "He was eating cake in the cafe.";
$matches = preg_match_all($pattern, $text, $array);
echo $matches . " matches were found.";
?>
```

Predefined Character Classes

There are certain character classes such as whitespaces, letters, and digits that are often used. As a result, they have shortcut names defined for them. The table below lists some of the predefined character classes:

Shortcut	Function
.	It matches a single character except for only a new line \n
\d	It matches any digit character. Similar to [0-9]
\D	It matches any non-digit character. Similar to [^0-9]
\s	It matches whitespace character. Similar to [\t\n\r]
\w	It will match any word character and underscore. Similar to [a-zA-Z_0-9]
\W	It will match any non-word character. Similar to [^a-zA-Z_0-9]

The example below shows how to find and replace space using a hyphen character in a string by applying a regular expression and PHP preg_replace () function.

```php
<?php
$pattern = "/\s/";
$replacement = "-";
$text = "Earth revolves around\nthe\tSun";
// Replace spaces, newlines and tabs
echo preg_replace($pattern, $replacement, $text);
echo "<br>";
// Replace only spaces
echo str_replace(" ", "-", $text);
?>
```

Repetition Quantifiers

The previous section looked at how you can match a single character in different ways. Well, let's say you want to match more than one character. For example, you may want to search for words that have one or more instances of the letter p. This is the point where quantifiers become important. Quantifiers describe the number of times a character in a regular expression should match. The table below shows several ways that one can quantify a specific pattern.

RegExp	What it Does
p+	Matches one or more occurrences of the letter p.
p*	Matches zero or more occurrences of the letter p.
p?	Matches zero or one occurrences of the letter p.
p{2}	Matches exactly two occurrences of the letter p.
p{2,3}	Matches at least two occurrences of the letter p, but not more than three occurrences of the letter p.
p{2,}	Matches two or more occurrences of the letter p.
p{,3}	Matches at most three occurrences of the letter p

The regular expression used in the example below splits the string at a comma, series of a comma, and a combination applying PHP preg_split () function.

```php
<?php
$pattern = "/[\s,]+/";
$text = "My favourite colors are red, green and blue";
$parts = preg_split($pattern, $text);

// Loop through parts array and display substrings
foreach($parts as $part){
    echo $part . "<br>";
}
?>
```

Position Anchors

There are specific cases that you might want to match at the start or end of a line, string or word. To achieve this, you can apply anchors. Two common anchors include the caret (^) which signals the start of a string and a $ sign that represents the end of a string.

RegExp	Function
^p	It will match the letter p at the start of a line
p$	It will match the letter p at the end of a line

The regular expression applied in the following example displays only names from the names array which begin with the letter "j" and the PHP preg_group () function.

```php
<?php
$pattern = "/^J/";
$names = array("Jhon Carter", "Clark Kent", "John Rambo");
$matches = preg_grep($pattern, $names);

// Loop through matches array and display matched names
foreach($matches as $match){
    echo $match . "<br>";
}
?>
```

Pattern Modifiers

A pattern modifier will allow a developer to respond to a pattern match. Pattern modifiers appear directly after the regular expression. If you want to look for a pattern in a case-insensitive way, for example, then you should use the I modify such as /pattern/I. The table below has some of the most commonly used pattern modifiers.

Modifier	What it Does
i	Makes the match case-insensitive manner.
m	Changes the behavior of ^ and $ to match against a newline boundary (i.e. start or end of each line within a multiline string), instead of a string boundary.
g	Perform a global match i.e. finds all occurrences.
o	Evaluates the expression only once.
s	Changes the behavior of . (dot) to match all characters, including newlines.
x	Allows you to use whitespace and comments within a regular expression for clarity.

The example below will demonstrate how you can carry out a global case-insensitive search by applying the i modifier and PHP preg_match_all () function.

Modifier	What it Does
i	Makes the match case-insensitive manner.
m	Changes the behavior of ^ and $ to match against a newline boundary (i.e. start or end of each line within a multiline string), instead of a string boundary.
g	Perform a global match i.e. finds all occurrences.
o	Evaluates the expression only once.
s	Changes the behavior of . (dot) to match all characters, including newlines.
x	Allows you to use whitespace and comments within a regular expression for clarity.

Word Boundaries

A word boundary character (\b) will help you identify the words that start and end with a pattern. For instance, the regexp /\bcar/ matches words that start with a pattern car and match cartoon, carrot, cart but cannot match Oscar.

In the same way, the regexp /car\b/ matches words that end with the pattern car, and match scar, supercar, Oscar but cannot match cart. Similarly, /\bcar\b/ matches words that start and end with the pattern car and that will only match the word car. This example will show words starting with the car in bold:

```php
<?php
$pattern = '/\bcar\w*/';
$replacement = '<b>$0</b>';
$text = 'Words begining with car: cart, carrot, cartoon.
Words ending with car: scar, oscar, supercar.';
echo preg_replace($pattern, $replacement, $text);
?>
```

Chapter 8

Files

Files are very important for saving information that is important for other programs, storing data without the database, and extracting remote web pages to allow local processing.

The PHP interface for I/O resembles that of C language but PHP is not very complicated. A file handle is a basic unit used to select a file to write or read. The connection to a specific file is identified by the handle. This connection is then used in completing the operation on the file. The focus of this chapter will be mostly on how to read, close, and manipulate file handles in PHP.

Opening a file in PHP

Before you can perform any actions inside a file, you must open the file. The fopen() is the PHP function used in opening a file. The basic syntax of this function includes:

    fopen(filename, mode)

This function accepts two parameters as shown above. The first parameter passed to the function describes the name of the file that you want to open while the second parameter describes the mode in which the file must be opened. For instance:

    <?php $handle = fopen("data.txt", "r"); ?>

Files can be opened in any of the modes shown below:

Modes	What it does
r	Open the file for reading only.
r+	Open the file for reading and writing.
w	Open the file for writing only and clears the contents of file. If the file does not exist, PHP will attempt to create it.
w+	Open the file for reading and writing and clears the contents of file. If the file does not exist, PHP will attempt to create it.
a	Append. Opens the file for writing only. Preserves file content by writing to the end of the file. If the file does not exist, PHP will attempt to create it.
a+	Read/Append. Opens the file for reading and writing. Preserves file content by writing to the end of the file. If the file does not exist, PHP will attempt to create it.
x	Open the file for writing only. Return FALSE and generates an error if the file already exists. If the file does not exist, PHP will attempt to create it.
x+	Open the file for reading and writing; otherwise it has the same behavior as 'x'.

If you attempt to open a file that does not exist, PHP will show a warning message. If you want to avoid this error message, make sure that you implement a simple validation process that determines whether a file or directory exists. Use the PHP function file_exists (). Below is an example of a simple check using PHP.

```php
<?php
$file = "data.txt";

// Check the existence of file
if(file_exists($file)){
    // Attempt to open the file
    $handle = fopen($file, "r");
} else{
    echo "ERROR: File does not exist.";
}
?>
```

Tip
Certain operations that take place in a file and directory are vulnerable to errors. Therefore, it is advised to apply the error checking method to check if an error has happened in your script and handle the errors in the right way.

Close a File using PHP fclose () function

Once you are done using a file, the next thing that you need to do is to close the file. The fclose() function is very handy when you want to close a file. The example below shows how fclose function is used to close a file.

```php
<?php
$file = "data.txt";

// Check the existence of file

if(file_exists($file)){
    // Open the file for reading
    $handle = fopen($file, "r") or die("ERROR: Cannot
    open the file.");

    /* Some code to be executed */

    // Closing the file handle
    fclose($handle);
} else{
    echo "ERROR: File does not exist.";
}
?>
```

Tip

While PHP automatically closes all open files when a script ends, it is advised to always close a file once you have finished doing all operations.

How to read from files using the PHP fread () Function

Since you know how to open and close files, this section will discuss how to read data written in a file. There are several PHP functions that can allow a person to read data from a file. These functions allow you to read from a single character until the end of the file in just one operation.

Read A Fixed Number Of Characters

Several characters from a file can be read using the fread () function. The general syntax of this function is as follows:

fread (file handle, length in bytes)

As you can see, this function accepts two parameter, a file handle and the size in bytes of data to read. The example shown below reads "30" bytes from the file called data.txt

The code below shows how to read data in a file using the fread function.

```php
<?php
$file = "data.txt";

// Check the existence of file
if(file_exists($file)){
    // Open the file for reading
    $handle = fopen($file, "r") or die("ERROR: Cannot
    open the file.");

    // Read fixed number of bytes from the file
    $content = fread($handle, "20");

    // Closing the file handle
    fclose($handle);

    // Display the file content
    echo $content;
} else{
    echo "ERROR: File does not exist.";
}
?>
```

Reading the Entire Contents of a File

You can use the fread () function together with the function filesize () to read the whole file at once. The filesize () function displays the size of a file in bytes. Notice the code below.

138

```php
<?php
$file = "data.txt";

// Check the existence of file
if(file_exists($file)){
    // Open the file for reading
    $handle = fopen($file, "r") or die("ERROR: Cannot
    open the file.");

    // Reading the entire file
    $content = fread($handle, filesize($file));

    // Closing the file handle
    fclose($handle);

    // Display the file content
    echo $content;
} else{
    echo "ERROR: File does not exist.";
}
?>
```

The easiest method to read the whole contents of a file using PHP is to use the function readfile (). This function will allow you to read the contents of a file without opening it.

Another method that does the same function is the file_get_contents () function. This PHP function will accept the name and path to a file and read the whole file into a string variable.

You can also read the whole details from a file using the PHP file () function. This function does the same function as file_get_contents () but it displays the contents of a file as an array of lines instead of a single string. Every element of the returned array resembles each line in a file.

When it comes to processing file data, you will need to iterate over the array by using the foreach loop.

Writing Files with the fwrite function

Apart from reading data in a file, one can create data to a file or append it using the PHP fwrite () function. Shown below is the function's general syntax.

Fwrite (file handle, string)

This function also accepts two parameters. Below is a simple code to show how you can use it.

```php
<?php
$file = "note.txt";

// String of data to be written
$data = "The quick brown fox jumps over the lazy dog.";

// Open the file for writing
$handle = fopen($file, "w") or die("ERROR: Cannot open
the file.");

// Write data to the file
fwrite($handle, $data) or die ("ERROR: Cannot write the
file.");

// Closing the file handle
fclose($handle);

echo "Data written to the file successfully.";
?>
```

In this code, if the "note.txt" file misses, PHP will create it automatically and write the data. However, if the file exists, PHP will delete the previous contents in the file before writing any new data. This means that if your goal is to simply append the file and maintain the previous contents, you need to use the mode in the above example.

Another alternative method is to use the file_put_contents () function. You don't need to open a file just to write data when you use this function. You just need to supply the name and path to the file and the data that you want to write in the file.

Renaming a File

In PHP, if you want to rename a file or directory, use the rename () function.

Remove Files

There are times you might want to remove a file. Don't hesitate because PHP has got you covered. The PHP unlink () function fulfills that.

Chapter 9

Session and Cookies

What is a cookie?

A file that has a size below 4KB is called a cookie. It can be found on the client's computer. The particular domain that it has been written from is the only way the cookies can be read. What this means is that if there is a cookie set in domain B, it cannot be read from domain D.

Cookies defined by a user can only be seen by the user alone. Many web browsers have the ability to deactivate a cookie and third-party cookies. If this happens, PHP responds by sending a token of the cookie in the URL.

How A Cookie Works

In the above diagram:

1. A page containing cookies has been requested by the user.

2. The cookie is then installed in the computer of the user by the server.

3. The rest of the page requests sent by the user reports to the cookie name and value.

Why and What Time to Use Cookies

- When you want to monitor the status of an application.

- When you want to customize the experience of the user.

- To track down the pages that a user visits.

Creating a Cookie

Below is a basic syntax used to create a cookie:

```php
<?php

setcookie(cookie_name, cookie_value, [expiry_time], [cookie_path], [domain], [secure], [httponly]);

?>
```

Let's review the basic syntax in detail:

- PHP setcookie refers to the function used in creating a cookie.

- Cookie_name contains the cookie's name.

- Cookie_value, as the name suggests, describes the value stored in the cookie.

- Cookie_path sets the path of the cookie on the server.

- Domain - It is also optional and you can use it to set up access to a cookie hierarchy.

- Secure - This is also optional. By default, it is false. It indicates that the https is where the cookie has been sent. In addition, it determines whether HTTP is set to false or true.

- Httponly – Optional and set to true.

Next, you need to see an example that uses cookies. To do this, you develop a basic program that will let you store a username in a cookie for ten seconds.

The following code represents the above representation.

```php
<?php
    setcookie("user_name", "Guru99", time()+ 60,'/'); //
    expires after 60 seconds
    echo 'the cookie has been set for 60 seconds';
?>
```

Retrieving the Value of a Cookie

If you want to retrieve the value of a cookie, use the following code:

```php
<?php
    print_r($_COOKIE);     //output the contents of the
    cookie array variable
?>
```

Tip

$_COOKIE defines a super global variable in PHP. The global variable stores the defined values and names of all cookies. The approximate number of value that it can store depends on the memory size set in php.in. However, 1GB is the default value.

How to delete a cookie?

If you would like to delete a cookie before it expires, then you need to adjust the time into a period that has expired.

Session

The server stores a global variable called a session.

Each session contains a unique ID that extracts values stored in the server. The cookie that holds the session's unique ID is stored on the computer of the user whenever a session is defined. If the browser of the client does not allow cookies, the URL displays a special session ID. Sessions are different from cookies because they can store a lot of information.

The values of the session can automatically be deleted when you close the browser. To store the values permanently on the computer, you must use a database. Similar to $_COOKIE array variables, variables of a session is stored in the $_SESSION array variables.

Why and When Should You Use Session

- A session will allow you to store important information in a secure manner on the server where attackers cannot modify them.

- Sessions are the best for passing values between web pages.

- If you need alternative cookies because a browser does not support cookies.

- Sessions are the best for storage of global variables in an efficient and secure manner.

- When creating shopping cart applications and other applications that need you to store temporary information that is larger than 4KB.

How to create a session?

The first thing to do in creating a session is to call the PHP session_start function and then store the values in the $_SESSION array variable. The method of creating and retrieving values from a session is pictured below.

```php
<?php

session_start(); //start the PHP_session function

if(isset($_SESSION['page_count']))
{
    $_SESSION['page_count'] += 1;
}
else
{
    $_SESSION['page_count'] = 1;
}
echo 'You are visitor number ' . $_SESSION['page_count'];

?>
```

Destroying a Session

All session variables are deleted by the function session_destroy ().
Apply the unset () function if you want to delete a single session item.
The following code demonstrates how you can apply both functions.

```php
<?php

session_destroy(); //destroy entire session

?>
<?php

unset($_SESSION['product']); //destroy product session
item

?>
```

146

Chapter 10

Advanced OOP

This chapter intends to extend on the advanced topic of object-oriented programming in PHP. In chapter 5, you learned some basics about classes and objects. This chapter will cover more topics in OOP.

Extending classes

If you think of a few things in this world, you will discover that a majority of them have a main type and a sub-type. For instance, there are human beings. Human beings can be classified into men and women. In this case, men and women are described as sub-type. Both of them share a lot of attributes. For example, both have a head and a leg. Additionally, both have faces, ears, toes, mouth, and many others. In addition, they do similar activities. Most people walk in the same way, work the same way, brush teeth in the same way as well as eat in the same manner.

Besides the many similarities that human beings can share, there are also certain differences between men and women.

Extending classes refers to the ability to collect and put all the common features into one parent class. In our previous example, our parent class is "Human" and the "child" refers to classes that inherit all the features of the parent. This can be represented in the code as shown below:

```
<?
class Human {
    public $numHeads = 1;
    public $numArms = 2;
    public $numLegs = 2;
    public $canHaveBabies = false;

    public function brushTeeth()
    {
        // lots of code here
    }
    public function goToWork()
    {
        // lots of code here
    }
    public function eatFood()
    {
        // lots of code here
    }
}

class Man extends Human {
    // Our "Human" default already has the correct default for
    // $canHaveBabies, but just in case the default ever changes later...
    public $canHaveBabies = false;
}

class Woman extends Human{
    public $canHaveBabies = true;
}

class ThreeLeggedMan extends Man {
    public $numLegs = 3;
}
?>
```

You should discover that the last class does not extend to human but extends to Man. But because a ThreeLeggedMan is a Man, and a Man is a Human, then it follows that a ThreeLeggedMan is a Human.

Method Overloading

In other programming languages, overloading implies that you have two different class methods that have the same name but separate arguments. For example:

```php
public function eatFood($whatFood)
{
  echo "Yum! Eating with bare hands is messy!";
}

public function eatFood($whatFood,$useAFork)
{
  if($useAFork)
  {
    echo "Yum! Eating with a fork is much cleaner!";
  }
  else
  {
    echo "Yum! Eating with bare hands is messy!";
  }
}
```

In PHP, overloading refers to a different thing and is a bit complicated. The above code will display an error related to declaring the same function. But the traditional concept of overloading is still useful and anyone can achieve it in PHP but in a different style. The PHP function func_get_args () becomes handy when it comes to method overloading. Let's assume that you have a function or a method class that appears this way:

```php
function myFunction()
{
}

// All of the three below calls are valid:
myFunction();
myFunction(123);
myFunction(123,"abc");
```

Accessors and Mutators

These terms are popularly referred to as "getters" and "setters" because of the type of function it performs. Accessors such as "getters" refer to functions which return the value of a class property and Mutators – "setters" describe functions that change the class property. There is nothing different about these functions. The functions are called "Mutators" and "Accessors" because of the type of function that they do. Below is an example.

```
class Human
{
    private $name;

    public function getName()
    {
        return $this->name();
    }

    public function setName($name)
    {
        $this->name = $name;
    }
}
```

Obviously, many people will ask this question, "Why can't you make $name a public property?" Well, the answer is tied to the correct programming practices. That recommends that all properties whether public, private or protected must be accessed or altered using these functions.

However, the same people will come and say, "All right, that is stupid. I am not going to do that". Well, no one is forcing you to do so. Remember, the right programming practices will help you create a code which other people can use as well as a change without having a complete understanding of how the whole code works.

Assume that your bread toaster breaks, and you realize that if you open it up and hold down the lever a little, the toaster will heat up and toast your bread. That is a solution. It might work. However, something that you don't know is that holding down that lever may, eventually, explode the toaster.

That is the same situation here. You might have a class property that has a name, and a function called changeName (). You may decide to change the property into a public property and again change it directly. Even though it is going to work at first, you don't know that you will need to also change other things in the system. Unless you change it manually, you should be ready to deal with all sorts of problems that will arise.

Therefore, you can see that Accessors and Mutators become even more important when you built a code that will be part of a large system. The more complex a code is, the more important these functions become.

The reason why you should use setters and getters is because they allow you to change values as they are processed. You could have an accessor function which returns the name of a person but also changes it into an upper-case first letter. A mutator function can select a value presented on the web and run it through various security checks before it can assign the sanitized value to the class property.

The_get Method

There are certain useful methods which you can define in your class to make it "smarter". Some of these methods exist in each class, but PHP can handle them by default. You can let PHP know that you want to handle that task yourself. All you need to do is to create a new class method using any special name.

The first method you can use is the _ get. This is a simple accessor function. If you attempt to get a property that doesn't exist, this function is called.

The _set Method

This is the opposite of the _get method. Rather than deal with the cases where the code is trying to access a property that doesn't exist, the _set method will handle instances which your code attempts to SET a missing property.

The _construct method

This method is called when you create a new class instance. Most people use this method to automatically run some extra code the moment the instance is created.

In closing, what this chapter has covered is just but a tip of an iceberg. PHP has a lot of flexibility in the way it handles classes.

Conclusion

Thank for making it through to the end of *PHP: A Comprehensive Intermediate Guide To Learn the Concept of PHP Programming*. Let's hope it was informative and able to provide you with all of the tools you need to achieve your goals whatever they may be.

Static sites are those built using HTML and CSS, and their content can only be updated by the site administrator. On the other hand, Dynamic sites are created using languages such as PHP and MYSQL plus a combination of HTML and CSS. These sites will allow visitors to participate by posting a message to make the site live. Visitors to a website are referred to as clients, and they request the server that hosts the site to send them web pages.

PHP is a language that is executed on the server. This book has covered different concepts in PHP: from how to use Restful APIs, create graphics in PHP, classes, and objects in PHP, and many others. You have also learned how you can use PHP cookies and session to pass data between different pages.

That is not enough because PHP is a powerful language and there are many things which you need to learn. This book provides you with a solid foundation to continue to explore other advanced PHP related topics. As such, don't stop learning because upgrades in PHP are released often, and it is advised to remain updated with what is taking place in the technology sector.

PHP

---

*Advanced Detailed Approach
to Master PHP Programming Language
for Web Development*

Introduction

This book aims to make you an expert in PHP. Being an expert in programming does not mean that you have mastered the syntax and properties of the language. It simply means you can use the language to create solutions to problems. Once you finish reading this book, you should have a good ground to expand your knowledge into deeper PHP concepts. Additionally, you should be in a better position to handle problems both inside and outside the web domain.

This book strives to be concept-focused by reviewing the general problems and applying examples as a demonstration. The purpose of this book is to present you the tools to use to solve any problem and the knowledge to select the right tool for the job.

It is easier to learn by example, and this book provides you practical examples that implement all the concepts that it discusses.

PHP is not a glue language that is applied by a small-time enthusiast. Instead, it has become a powerful scripting language whose design is perfect for solving problems in the web domain.

Chapter 1

Styles of Coding in PHP

Regardless of your PHP proficiency, regardless of how far you have mastered the language internals or the syntaxes, it is easy to create a sloppy code. A hard-to-read code is difficult to manage and debug. A poor coding style demonstrates a lack of professionalism.

If you were to remain at work for the entire period of your life, and no one else had to manage your code, it will still not be okay to create a poorly structured code. It is difficult to troubleshoot or augment libraries that you wrote two or even three years ago. It will always take time to understand the logic.

To worsen the situation, no one codes in a vacuum. The codes require to be maintained by current and future peers. The merging of two independently readable styles can be unreadable and left without maintenance such that there is no style guide at all. As a result, it is important that we apply a style that anyone can understand, and the style should be consistent across all the developers collaborating.

Picking a style that is right for you

When it comes to choosing a style to code, you need to consider it carefully. Keep in mind that the code lives past us, and changing a style later is more challenging than it is worth. Code that includes different styles with every new developer can quickly turn into a mess.

The same way it is important to select a new style in a project that has none, you also need to beware of other standards. Remember, there is no perfect standard. The preference of someone determines a coding style. Much more important than selecting "the perfect style" is picking a consistent style across all your code. You should not be too quick to change a consistent style you do not like.

The code format and layout

This includes indentation, the use of whitespace, line length, and application of Structured Query Language (SQL), which is the most basic tool you can apply to cement the logical structure of your code.

Indentation

This book will apply indentation to arrange the code and represent blocks of code. The significance of indentation for code organization cannot be exaggerated. Most programmers take it seriously that the Python Scripting language applies indentation as the syntax; if the Python code isn't indented correctly, the program will not parse.

While in PHP, indentation is not a prerequisite; it is still a great visual organization tool that you need to use in your code always.

See the following code:

```
if($month == 'september' || $month == 'april' || $month == 'june' || $month ==
'november') { return 30;
}
else if($month == 'february') {
if((($year % 4 == 0) && !($year % 100)) || ($year % 400 == 0)) {
return 29;
}
else {
return 28;
}
}
else {
return 31;
}
```

Now, compare that with this block of code that is identical, apart from the indentation.

```php
if($month == 'september' ||
$month == 'april' ||
$month == 'june' ||
$month == 'november') {
return 30;
}
else if($month == 'february') {
if((($year % 4 == 0) && ($year % 100)) || ($year % 400 == 0)) {
return 29;
}
else {
return 28;
}
}
else {
return 31;
}
```

In the last version, it is easier to differentiate the flow of logic than in the first version.

When you use tabs to indent your code, you need to make a firm decision whether the tabs should be soft or hard. Hard tabs refer to regular tabs. On the other hand, soft tabs aren't tabs at all. Each soft tab is defined with a specific number of regular spaces. The advantage of applying soft tabs is that they always appear similar no matter what the setting of the editor's tab-spacing is. Most people prefer to use soft tabs. When the soft tabs are set, it is easy to ensure consistency in indentation and whitespace application in the entire code. When you enforce hard tabs, especially when multiple developers are working on different editors, it is easy for different levels of indentation to be created.

You also need to select the tab width that you want to apply. A tab width of four spaces displays a code that is easy to read and offers a reasonable amount of nesting. Since book pages are a bit smaller than terminal windows, you should apply two space tab-widths.

Most PHP editors allow auto-detection of formatting based on "magic" comments in the source code. In most big projects, these types of comments are positioned at the bottom of each file to make sure developers follow the indentation rules of the project.

```
/*
* Local variables:
* tab-width: 2
* c-basic-offset: 2
* indent-tabs-mode: nil
* End:
*/
```

Length of a line

For long lines, it is easy to get confused. Therefore, you need to consider dividing the line. Here is an example of a code snippet that is split.

For example:

```
if($month == 'september' || $month == 'april' ||
$month == 'june' || $month == 'november') {
return 30;
}
```

If you want, you can decide to indent the second line to represent the relationship with the first line. So it can be:

```
if($month == 'september' ||
$month == 'april' ||
$month == 'june' ||
$month == 'november')
{
return 30;
}
```

The same concept applies to functions.

```
mail("postmaster@example.foo",
"My Subject",
$message_body,
"From: George Schlossnagle <george@owako.com>\r\n");
```

Overall, lines that have more than 80 characters should be divided.

Application of Whitespace

You can apply whitespace in your code to improve the logical structure of a program. For example, whitespace can be used to collect assignments and show the relation. This example has been formatted poorly and is hard for a person to read.

```
$lt = localtime();
$name = $_GET['name'];
$email = $_GET['email'];
$month = $lt['tm_mon'] + 1;
$year = $lt['tm_year'] + 1900;
$day = $lt['tm_day'];
$address = $_GET['address'];
```

In this particular code, you can use whitespace to make it look better. See the code below:

```
$name = $_GET['name'];
$email = $_GET['email'];
$address = $_GET['address'];

$lt = localtime();
$day = $lt['tm_day'];
$month = $lt['tm_mon'] + 1;
$year = $lt['tm_year'] + 1900;
```

SQL Guidelines

Both the formatting and layout rules discussed so far apply to PHP and SQL code. In the modern web architectures, Databases are a consistent aspect. As a result, SQL is common in most of the code bases. SQL queries support the writing of complex subqueries.

Consider this query:

```
$query = "SELECT FirstName, LastName FROM employees, departments WHERE
employees.dept_id = department.dept_id AND department.Name = 'Engineering'";
```

This query has been poorly written. However, you can rearrange it in different ways by making the following changes:

1. Capitalize keywords

2. Use table aliases to make the code clean

3. Break the lines on keywords

Here is how you can apply the changes in an SQL query:

```
$query = "SELECT firstname,

    lastname

FROM employees e,

  departments d

WHERE u.dept_id = d.dept_id

AND d.name = 'Engineering'";
```

Control flow constructs

These are critical features of the modern programming languages. The control flow constructs always regulate the order in which the program execution follows. There are two kinds of control flow constructs:

1. Conditionals

2. Loops

A condition includes statements that are only executed once a specific condition is met. On the other hand, the loop is statements executed in a repeated fashion.

The power to test and execute condition statements allows for logic implementation and making decisions in code. Alternatively, loops will make it possible for one to run the same logic repeatedly, solving complex problems on unknown data.

The use of braces in control structures

PHP borrows most of its syntax from the C programming language. In the C language, a single-line conditional statement does not need to have a brace. The same applies to PHP.

For instance, this code will run without any issues:

```php
if(isset($name))

echo "Hello $name";
```

Even if this is the valid syntax, you should never apply it. When you exclude braces, you make it hard to change the code later without making mistakes. For instance, if you wanted to include an extra line to this particular example, where *$name* is set, and you don't pay attention, you may easily write this way:

```php
if(isset($name))

    echo "Hello $name";
    $known_user = true;
```

The above code will not perform what you expected it to do. The *$known_user* is unconditionally set to true, although you intended to set it only if *$name* had also been set. Thus, to fix such problems, you need to use braces in your code always, even if you only have a single statement that is conditionally executed.

```php
if(isset($name)) {
    echo "Hello $name";
}
else {
    echo "Hello Stranger";
}
```

Consistent use of braces

It is important to have a consistent means for using braces toward the end of the conditionals. Here are some of the methods that you can choose to use:

1. BSD style. For this method, the braces match with the keyword after the condition.

```
if ($condition)
{

// statement
}
```

2. GNU style.

```
if ($condition)
    {

        // statement
    }
```

3. K&R style. For this particular style, the first brace appears on the same line as the keyword:

```
if ($condition){

        // statement
    }
```

The story of brace style is like the history of religion. The type of brace style to pick is not that important; you only need to choose one and apply it throughout your coding. The most important thing is consistency.

Also, when you work on a project with a different style guide from the one you prefer, you should always stick to the one used in the project.

for while and foreach

Do not use a *while* loop where you can use a *for* or *foreach* loop. Take this code for example:

```
function is_prime($number)
{

$i = 2;
while($i < $number) {
    if ( ($number % $i ) == 0) {
  return false;
    }
    $i++;
}
return true;
}
```

The loop in the above program is not that robust. Compare that with the next code:

```
function is_prime($number)
{
  If(($number % 2) != 0) {
    return true;
  }
  $i = 0;
  while($i < $number) {
    // A cheap check to see if $i is even
    if( ($i & 1) == 0 ) {
      continue;
    }
    if ( ($number % $i ) == 0) {
      return false;
    }
    $i++;
  }
return true;
}
```

In this code, test the number to see if it is divisible by 2. If it is true, no need to try out to see if it is divisible by any even number. You would have unintentionally preempted the increment operation and will loop forever.

The application of **for** loop makes it natural for the iteration. For example:

```
function is_prime($number)
{
   if(($number % 2) != 0) {
      return true;
   }
   for($i=0; $i < $number; $i++) {
      // A cheap check to see if $i is even
      if( ($i & 1) == 0 ) {
         continue;
      }
      if ( ($number % $i ) == 0) {
         return false;
      }
   }
   return true;
}
```

When you loop through arrays, what is even more effective than using **for** is applying the *foreach* operator. For example:

```
$array = (3, 5, 10, 11, 99, 173);
foreach($array as $number) {
   if(is_prime($number)) {
print "$number is prime.\n";
   }

}
```

This particular code will run faster than a **for** loop because it doesn't have an explicit counter.

Break and continue statement

While implementing logic in a loop, you can decide to include break statements to exit blocks when you don't need to be there. See the code below:

```
$has_ended = 0;
while(($line = fgets($fp)) !== false) {
    if($has_ended) {
    }
    else {
        if(strcmp($line, '_END_') == 0) {
            $has_ended = 1;
        }
        if(strncmp($line, '//', 2) == 0) {
        }
        else {
            // parse statement
        }
    }
}
```

In this particular code, you want to ignore lines that begin with the C++ comment style and stop parsing once you click an _END_ declaration. If you don't apply the flow control approach inside the loop, you will be forced to create a small state machine. You can prevent this poor nesting if you include *continue* and *break* statement. Here is an example:

```
while(($line = fgets($fp)) !== false) {
    if(strcmp($line, '_END_') == 0) {
        break;
    }
    if(strncmp($line, '//', 2) == 0) {
        continue;
    }

    // parse statement

}
```

This example is shorter than the previous one and also eliminates the confusion of deep-nested logic.

How to avoid the deeply nested loops?

Another popular mistake that programmers make is writing deeply nested loops when a shallow loop would have done so. Below is a common example of code that demonstrates the mistake.

```
$fp = fopen("file", "r");
if ($fp) {
    $line = fgets($fp);
    if($line !== false) {
        // process $line
    } else {
        die("Error: File is empty);
    }
}
else { die("Error: Couldn't open file");
}
```

In this code, the main body begins two indentation levels. This creates confusion and may lead to longer lines, which creates error-handling conditions in the entire block and makes it easy for one to make nesting errors.

A straightforward way is to fix all errors up front and avoid unnecessary nesting. For example:

```
$fp = fopen("file", "r");
if (!$fp) {
  die("Couldn't open file");
}
$line = fgets($fp);
if($line === false) {
die("Error: Couldn't open file");
}
// process $line
```

Naming symbols

PHP language contains symbols used to relate data with the names of variables. Symbols create a means for naming data for reuse by a program. Any moment you define and declare a variable, you always create an entry in the existing symbol table for it to be related to its current value. For example:

$num = 'vehicle';

This variable declaration writes an entry into the current symbol table for *num* and connects it to the current value, *vehicle*. Alternatively, once you create class or function, you always insert the class into a different symbol table. See another example:

```
function hello($name)
{

print "Hello $name\n";

}
```

In this example, hello is inserted into a different symbol table, the one for functions, and connected to the compiled optree for its code.

The names of functions and variables fill the PHP code. Just like a great layout, naming schemes serve a similar purpose of improving the code logic for the reader. Most large projects have their own naming scheme to ensure that their code is consistent. The rules discussed here are from the PHP Extension and Application Repository (PEAR) guideline style.

PEAR is a composition of PHP codes and classes created to support reusability and fulfill certain popular needs. Since it is the largest public repository of PHP codes and classes, PEAR offers an efficient standard for reference. And this is where the first rule of variable naming arises: Don't use names that don't make sense for variables. Although plenty of computer resources use nonsense variable names that don't add any meaning to the reader, you should avoid doing the same.

Take a look at this code:

```php
function test($baz)
{

for($foo = 0; $foo < $baz; $foo++) {
    $bar[$foo] = "test_$foo";
}
return $bar;
}
```

This code can be swapped with a meaningful code that has variable names that make sense. So you can understand what is happening:

```php
function create_test_array($size)
{

    for($i = 0; $i < $size; $i++) {
        $retval[$i] = "test_$i";
    }

return $retval;
}
```

In the PHP language, variables declared outside a function or a class are referred to as global variables. Any variable that is defined inside a function is only accessible to that function.

For global variables, they have to be declared using the *global* keyword for them to be accessible within a function.

These rules that govern how you can access variables where you declared them are referred to as the rules of scope.

A variable's scope is one that can be accessed without advances steps to access it. While these rules of scoping look simple, they make the naming guidelines that define whether a variable is global. You can divide PHP variables into three types of variables that can adhere to separate naming conventions:

- **Truly global**: These are variables that you want to refer to a global scope.

- **Long-lived:** These variables can be defined in any scope but carry important information.

- **Temporary:** These variables are applied in small sections of code and carry temporary information.

Truly global variables and constants

These require to be in capital letters. And this ensures that it is easy to notice them as global variables.

```
$CACHE_PATH = '/var/cache/';
...
function list_cache()
{
  global $CACHE_PATH;
  $dir = opendir($CACHE_PATH);
  while(($file = readdir($dir)) !== false && is_file($file)) {
    $retval[] = $file;
  }
closedir($dir);
return $retval;
  }
```

When you use all-uppercase for truly global variables and constants, you can easily know when you are globalizing a variable that you shouldn't globalize.

Applying global variables in PHP is a huge mistake. Overall, global variables aren't good because of the following:

- They can easily be changed from any place. This makes the process of debugging more difficult.

- They contaminate the global namespace. If you apply a global variable together with a generic name like $counter and you use a library that also contains a global variable $counter, each will hit the other. As the codebases grow, this conflict becomes difficult to avoid.

The solution is to apply an accessor function rather than use a global variable for any the variables in a consistent database connection like in this example:

```
global $database_handle;
global $server;
global $user;
global $password;
$database_handle = mysql_pconnect($server, $user, $password);
```

You can decide to use a class. See the following code:

173

```
class Mysql_Test {
 public $database_handle;
 private $server = 'localhost';
 private $user = 'test';
 private $password = 'test';
 public function __construct()
 {

 $this->database_handle =
   mysql_pconnect($this->server, $this->user, $this->password);
  }
}
```

Sometimes, you may want to access a specific variable like the following:

```
$US_STATES = array('Alabama', ... , 'Wyoming');
```

In the above example, a class is a perfect solution for the task. If you want to eliminate a global here, you can include an accessor function that contains a global array as a static variable:

```
function us_states()
{
    static $us_states = array('Alabama', ... , 'Wyoming');
return $us_states;

}
```

This method has the advantage of changing the source code array to become immutable like it has been set with *define*.

Long-lived variables

These variables should have a brief but descriptive name. A descriptive name improves readability and simplifies the process of tracking variables in a large project. In this example, the descriptive variable names demonstrate the intention and action of the code:

174

```
function clean_cache($expiration_time)
  $cachefiles = list_cache();
  foreach($cachefiles as $cachefile) {
    if(filemtime($CACHE_PATH."/".$cachefile) > time() +
    $expiration_time) {
unlink($CACHE_PATH."/".$cachefile);
    }
  }
}

}
```

Temporary variables

These variables should be short and brief. Since temporary variables exist only inside a small block of code, there is no need for them to have explanatory names. Specifically, numeric variables applied in iteration should be described as I, j, k, and n.

Compare the following example:

```
$number_of_parent_indices = count($parent);
for($parent_index=0; $parent_index <$number_of_parent_indices; $parent_index++) {
$number_of_child_indices = count($parent[$parent_index]);
for($child_index = 0; $child_index < $number_of_child_indices; $child_index++) {
my_function($parent[$parent+index][$child_index]);
}
}
```

With the following:

```
$pcount = count($parent);
  for($i = 0; $i < $pcount; $i++) {
    $ccount = count($parent[$i]);
    for($j = 0; $j < $ccount; $j++) {
        my_function($parent[$i][$j]);
    }
}
```

Multi-word names

Two schools of thought direct the handling of word breaks in multi-word variable names. Some people prefer a combination to represent the breaks. See this example:

```
$numElements = count($elements);
```

The other technique is to apply underscores to break words. For instance:

```
$num_elements = count($elements);
```

The second method for naming variables and functions is better because of the following:

- There is a meaning for the phrase Case in truly global variables and constants. To ensure there is consistency in the difference, you will need to create multi-word names that resemble $CACHEDIR and $PROFANITYMACROSET.

- A lot of databases have a case-insensitive name for schema items. If you want to match the names of the variable to database column names, you will still experience concatenation challenges in the database that you work with the global names.

- It is easy to read underscore-delimited names.

- For nonnative English speakers, they will consider searching for variable names in a dictionary easier in case the words are broken explicitly with underscores.

Function names

Function names should be dealt in the same way that normal program variable names are handled. First, they should appear in lowercase, and multi-word names should have an underscore to distinguish them. Additionally, you should try to use K&R brace styling for function declarations, putting the bracket below the function keyword. This is different from the K&R style for positioning braces concerning conditionals. Take a look at a classic example of K&R styling:

```
function print_hello($name)
{

echo "Hello $name";

}
```

Quality names

Other programmers should understand a code written in any language. The variable of a function or class should describe exactly what the symbol is meant to do. By naming a function bar() or foo () does not improve the readability of the code. Besides that, it is unprofessional and makes it hard to maintain the code.

Names of classes

The names of classes should adhere to the following rules:

1. The first letter of a class name has to be in uppercase letters. This differentiates the name of a class from its members.

2. Underscores should be applied as a way to simulate nested namespaces.

3. Multi-word class names should have the first word of every letter capitalized.

Below is an example that demonstrates this guideline:

```
class XML_RSS {}
class Text_PrettyPrinter {}
```

Method names

Words should be concatenated in multi-word method names and capitalize the first letter of every word after the first. Here is an example:

```
class XML_RSS
{

function startHandler() {}

}
```

Naming consistency

Variables used for the same functions should share names. A code that appears this way illustrates problems.

```
$num_elements = count($elements);
...
$objects_cnt = count($objects);
```

In case a single naming scheme is chosen, there is no need to scan through the code to verify that you are using the correct variable name. Other popular qualifies that is nice to standardize include:

```
$max_elements;
$min_elements;
$sum_elements;
$prev_item;
$curr_item;
$next_item;
```

Chapter 2

Object-Oriented Programming using Design Patterns

One of the largest and significant changes in PHP5 is the complete redefinition of the object model and the highly enhanced support for modern object-oriented (OO) techniques and methodologies. This chapter will not focus on OO programming techniques nor design patterns. However, there are resourceful sources for this particular information. You can try to check on PHP websites. This chapter will briefly focus on the OO features in PHP5 and a few popular design patterns. This chapter will briefly explore the advanced features of OO present in PHP.

OO programming is the new paradigm after procedural programming. As you all know, procedural programming is the traditional methodology for PHP programmers. In procedural programming, data is kept in variables that you can pass to functions, which process the data and can change it or build new data. A procedural program is just like a list of commands that are executed in a certain order using functions, control statements, and so forth. Here is a look of a procedural program:

```php
<?php
function hello($name)
{
    return "Hello $name!\n";
}
function goodbye($name)
{
    return "Goodbye $name!\n";
}
function age($birthday) {
    $ts = strtotime($birthday);
    if($ts === -1) {
        return "Unknown";
    }
    else {
        $diff = time() - $ts;
        return floor($diff/(24*60*60*365));
    }
}
$name = "george";
$bday = "10 Oct 1973";
echo hello($name);
echo "You are ".age($bday)." years old.\n";
echo goodbye($name);
?>
```

Introduction to OO programming

It is critical to understand that when it comes to procedural programming, both the data and functions are set aside from each other. But in OO programming, data is linked with objects. An object is defined based on the instance of the class it belongs to. A class describes the attributes or properties that an object holds, plus the methods it may apply. An object is created once you instantiate the class.

Instantiation results in a new object; it initializes all the attributes and calls its constructor, which is a function that runs any setup operations.

A constructor of a class in PHP has to be named using _ _ *constructor* () so that the compiler can know how to describe it. This program creates a class User, instantiates the class, and calls the two methods of the class.

```php
<?php
class User {
    public $name;
    public $birthday;
    public function _ _construct($name, $birthday)
{

    $this->name = $name;
    $this->birthday = $birthday;
}
public function hello()
{
    return "Hello $this->name \n";
}
public function goodbye()
{
    return "Goodbye $this->name \n";
}
public function age() {
    $ts = strtotime($this->birthday);
    if($ts === -1) {
        return "Unknown";
    }
else {
    $diff = time() - $ts;
    return floor($diff/(24*60*60*365)) ;
    }
    }
}
$user = new User('george', '10 Oct 1973');
echo $user->hello();
echo "You are " $user->age() ." years old.\n";
echo $user->goodbye();
?>
```

The constructor used in this code is basic because what it does is initialize two attributes: birthday and name. The methods are, again, simple. Remember that $this is created automatically within the class methods, and it defines the User object. If you want to access a method or property, you need to apply the -> notation.

Outside, an object does not look different from an associative array and a collection of functions that work on it. Though there are extra properties explained here:

- **Inheritance_** This is the ability to extract a new class from the current ones and override their properties and methods.

- **Encapsulation_** This is a means of hiding data from users of the class.

- **Special methods_** As said before; classes support constructors that can do setup work once a new object is defined. They still have event callbacks that are started on other common events such as on copy, on destruction, and so forth.

- **Polymorphism_** If two classes execute the same external methods, they have to be used interchangeably in functions. Since this is a huge topic that requires a larger knowledge base than you currently hold, we will not discuss it in this chapter.

Inheritance

If you want to create a new class with similar attributes of the main class, then you need to use inheritance. In PHP, you can extend a class to a current class. Once a class is extended, the new class has the same properties as the parent class. Still, it is possible to define new methods and properties for your new class and override the existing ones. The keyword extends is used to define inheritance.

182

Here is an example:

```php
class AdminUser extends User{
    public $password;
    public function _ _construct($name, $birthday)
    {
        parent::_ _construct($name, $birthday);
        $db = dba_popen("/data/etc/auth.pw", "r", "ndbm");
        $this->password = dba_fetch($db, $name);
        dba_close($db);
    }
    public function authenticate($suppliedPassword)
    {

        if($this->password === $suppliedPassword) {
            return true;
    }

        else {
            return false;
        }
    }
}
```

Encapsulation

Users of a procedural language may wonder what all the public staff in OO programming is. The PHP5 offers data-hiding ability using the private, public, and protected data properties. Sometimes they are described as PPP.

Encapsulation permits you to describe a public interface that controls how users interact with a class. You can modify methods that are not public, without feeling worried about interfering with the code that uses the class. You can alter private methods with liberty. The modification of private methods demands a lot of care so that you don't destroy the subclass of the classes.

Encapsulation is not important in PHP, in case it is removed, then methods and properties are said to be public, but it should be applied where possible. Still, in a single-programmer environment and particular

183

team environments, the desire to eliminate the public interface of a specific object and go for a shortcut by including internal methods is normally high. This will rapidly result in unmaintainable code, and that is because rather than a simple public interface being consistent, methods in a class cannot be altered because of the fear of a bug. However, the application of PPP ties you to the following agreement and verifies that only public methods are applied by the external code, regardless of the desire to use a shortcut.

Static attributes and methods

PHP methods and properties can be declared as static. A static method is one that is tied to a class instead of the instance of the class. Static methods are called by applying the syntax ClassName::method (). Within the static methods, $this is not present.

A static property is described as one in which the class variable is connected with the class, instead of an instance of the class. This implies that when it is modified, the change happens in all instances of the class. Static properties are defined using the static keyword and are accessed using the syntax ClassName::$property. This example demonstrates how static properties work.

```
class TestClass {
public static $counter;
}
$counter = TestClass::$counter;
```

If you want to access a static property within a class, you can still apply the magic keywords *self* and *parent,* which evaluate to the current class and the parent of the existing class. By applying self and parent, it makes you eliminate explicit referencing the class using the name. Here is an example that applies the static property to allocate a unique integer ID to each instance of the class.

184

```
class TestClass {
  public static $counter = 0;
  public $id;

  public function _ _construct()
{
   $this->id = self::$counter++;
   }
}
```

Special methods

Classes in PHP reserve specific method names as unique callbacks to deal with specific events. You have already observed _ _construct (), which is called automatically once an object is instantiated. Classes include the five other unique callbacks: _ _get (), _ _ call (), and _ _ set () affect how the class properties and methods are called. The remaining two include _ _destruct () and _ _ clone ().

_ _ destruct () refers to the callback for object destruction. Destructors are important for closing important resources that a class develops. In the PHP language, variables are *reference counted.*

Once the variable reference counts hit 0, the variable is excluded from the system using a garbage collector. In case this variable is an object, its _ _ destruct () method is called.

Take a look at this small PHP file wrapper to illustrate destructors:

185

```
class IO {
  public $fh = false;
  public function _ _construct($filename, $flags)
{
    $this->fh = fopen($filename, $flags);
}
public function _ _destruct()
{
    if($this->fh) {
  }
}
public function read($length)
{
    if($this->fh) {
return fread($this->fh, $length);
  }
 }
}
/* ... */
}
```

Most of the time, building a destructor isn't important because PHP reviews the resources when the request completes. For scripts that run for a long time or scripts that open a huge number of files, aggressive resource cleanup is critical.

For PHP4, the objects are passed by value. In other words, if you executed the following in PHP4:

```
$obj = new TestClass;
$copy = $obj;
```

Then you will require three copies for the class.

- The first class in the constructor

- Another one at the assignment of the return value

- And when you transfer $copy to $obj

Introduction to design patterns

When it comes to design patterns, you must have come across them; the only difference is that you didn't know what they are. Design patterns can be considered as a general solution to a set of problems that software developers experience often.

If you have programmed for quite some time, then you have experienced a situation where you need to use a library that can be accessed with an alternative API. This is a common problem that all developers experience. While there is no specific general solution, developers succeed to identify the problem. The main concept behind design patterns is that problems plus the corresponding solutions follow a given repeatable pattern.

Problems exist in design patterns because they are patterns that have been overhyped. They present a set of vocabulary for identifying a problem and classifying the same problems. The deities and entities in Egyptian mythology had unique names that were very secretive. If you did manage to discover those names, you would acquire the power to control the deities and entities. Well, you may wonder why we are talking about deities and entities in ancient Egypt. It is because design patterns behave in the same manner. If you can discover the true nature of a problem and connect it with a known set of solutions, you are on the correct path to solving it.

A design pattern is a huge topic that everything cannot be covered in a single chapter. However, we shall look at some of the design patterns.

Adaptor Pattern

This is used to deliver access to an object through a specific interface. In an advanced OO language, the Adaptor pattern mainly handles the provision of a different API to an object. However, PHP considers this pattern as creating an alternative interface to a set of procedural routines.

Paving the way to interface with a class through a set of API can be useful for two major reasons:

- If multiple classes that offer the same services execute the same API, you can shift between the classes during runtime. This is defined as polymorphism. It is drawn from the Latin word poly that means "many" and morph that means "form."

- A predefined structure for working on a set of objects could be difficult to alter.

When you include a third-party class that doesn't adhere to the API applied in the predefined structure, it is easier to involve an Adaptor to create access through the expected API.

The most popular application of adaptors in PHP isn't building an alternative interface to one class through another. PHP holds the properties of a procedural language, and hence, most of the built-in PHP functions are procedural.

When you want to access functions sequentially, say you are building a database query, you have to apply:

```
mysql_pconnect(), mysql_select_db(),
mysql_query(), and mysql_fetch())
```

A resource always stores the connection data, and you direct that into your functions. Wrapping this whole process into a class can assist most of the repetitive work and error handling that is required to be done.

The concept is to encompass an object interface around the two main MYSQL extension resources: the resource for connection and the result resource. The purpose is not to create a true abstraction but to generate sufficient wrapper code that you can use all the MYSQL extension functions in an OO way and include some extra convenience. Here is an example of that wrapper class:

```
class DB_Mysql {
  protected $user;
  protected $pass;
  protected $dbhost;
  protected $dbname;
  protected $dbh; // Database connection handle

public function __construct($user, $pass, $dbhost, $dbname) {
  $this->user = $user;
  $this->pass = $pass;
  $this->dbhost = $dbhost;
  $this->dbname = $dbname;
}
protected function connect() {
  $this->dbh = mysql_pconnect($this->dbhost, $this->user, $this->pass);
  if(!is_resource($this->dbh)) {
     throw new Exception;
}
if(!mysql_select_db($this->dbname, $this->dbh)) {
   throw new Exception;
  }
}
public function execute($query) {
  if(!$this->dbh) {
    $this->connect();
}
```

```
if(!$ret) {
  throw new Exception;
  }
  else if(!is_resource($ret)) {
    return TRUE;
} else {
  $stmt = new DB_MysqlStatement($this->dbh, $query);
  $stmt->result = $ret;
  return $stmt;
  }
 }
}
```

Template pattern

This defines a class that alters the logic of a subclass to complete it.

Template pattern is best used to hide all the database operations. If you want to use the class from the previous section, you have to describe the connection parameters.

189

```php
<?php
require_once 'DB.inc';

define('DB_MYSQL_PROD_USER', 'test');
define('DB_MYSQL_PROD_PASS', 'test');
define('DB_MYSQL_PROD_DBHOST', 'localhost');
define('DB_MYSQL_PROD_DBNAME', 'test');

$dbh = new DB::Mysql(DB_MYSQL_PROD_USER, DB_MYSQL_PROD_PASS,
          DB_MYSQL_PROD_DBHOST, DB_MYSQL_PROD_DBNAME);
$stmt = $dbh->execute("SELECT now()");
print_r($stmt->fetch_row());
?>
```

To eradicate the need to define your connection parameters always, you can decide to subclass DB_Mysql and then do some hard code for the connection part of the test database:

```php
class DB_Mysql_Test extends DB_Mysql {
   protected $pass = "testpass";
   protected $dbhost = "localhost";
   protected $dbname = "test";


public function _ _construct() { }
}
```

Alternatively, you can do the same thing if you want for the production instance.

Polymorphism

The database wrappers used in this chapter are more general. In fact, when you consider other database extensions developed in PHP, you will notice the same basic functionality. If you prefer, you can create the same DB_Pgsql class that encloses the PostgreSQL, and you will still have the same methods inside.

While having the same methods do not add anything, the presence of identical methods to execute the same type of tasks is crucial. It will support polymorphism. This is the ability to substitute a single object transparently with another if the access APIs are similar.

Practically, polymorphism means you can define functions this way:

```
function show_entry($entry_id, $dbh)
{
    $query = "SELECT * FROM Entries WHERE entry_id = :1";
    $stmt = $dbh->prepare($query)->execute($entry_id);
    $entry = $stmt->fetch_row();
// display entry
}
```

Not only does this function work if the *$dbh* is a *DB_Mysql* object, but it also works well, provided that $dbh executes a *prepare ()* method and that particular method outputs an object that runs the *execute ()* and *fetch_assoc ()* methods.

To eliminate the chance of passing a database object into each function called, you can decide to apply the idea of delegation. Delegation is a concept in OO pattern where an object contains similar attributes as another object that uses it to run specific tasks.

The wrapper libraries for the database are a great example to demonstrate a class that is always delegated to. In a normal application, most of the classes required to execute database operations. The classes have two options:

- You can natively execute the database calls. But this is useless because it means all the efforts you have used to compile a database wrapper is pointless.

- You can apply the database wrapper API, but you have to instantiate objects immediately. See an example that includes this option:

```
class Weblog {
  public function show_entry($entry_id)
  {
    $query = "SELECT * FROM Entries WHERE entry_id = :1";
    $dbh = new Mysql_Weblog();
    $stmt = $dbh->prepare($query)->execute($entry_id);
    $entry = $stmt->fetch_row();
// display entry
  }
}
```

To instantiate a database connection immediately looks like an easy concept, but the challenge is that if you want to shift the database this class is using, you may need to follow through and change each function where a connection is done.

You can execute delegation by letting weblog hold a database wrapper object as a property of the class. Once an instance of a class is instantiated, it builds a database wrapper object that it will include for all input and output. Take a look at how to reimplement a weblog that applies the following technique:

```
class Weblog {
  protected $dbh;

  public function setDB($dbh)
  {
$this->dbh = $dbh;
}
  public function show_entry($entry_id)
  {
    $query = "SELECT * FROM Entries WHERE entry_id = :1";
    $stmt = $this->dbh->prepare($query)->execute($entry_id);
    $entry = $stmt->fetch_row();
    // display entry
  }
}
```

Next, you can set the database object this way:

```
$blog = new Weblog;
$dbh = new Mysql_Weblog;
$blog->setDB($dbh);
```

Still, you can decide to include a Template pattern to create a database delegate:

```
class DB_Mysql_Test extends DB_Mysql {
    protected $pass = "testpass";
    protected $dbhost = "localhost";
    protected $dbname = "test";


    public function _ _construct() { }
}
```

Delegation is crucial any time you have to execute a complex service that is likely to change inside a class. Another area where delegation is often applied is in classes that require to generate output.

Interfaces and type hints

A major factor to successful delegation is to make sure that all classes that could be released are polymorphic. In case you set as the $dbh parameter for the *weblog* object at a class that does not execute *fetch_row ()*, a fatal error is displayed at runtime. To detect runtime error is difficult, without verifying manually that all objects execute the requisite functions.

To track down these types of errors early, PHP5 brings the concept of interfaces. An interface resembles a skeleton of a class. It defines whichever number of methods, but it offers no code for them, only a prototype. Below is a basic *interface* that defines the methods required for a database connection.

```
interface DB_Connection {
  public function execute($query);
  public function prepare($query);


}
```

Inheritance in a class occurs by extending it, with an interface. There is no code defined; you just agree to execute the functions.

For instance:

DB_Mysql executes all the function prototypes defined by *DB_Connection* so that you can declare like this:

```
class DB_Mysql implements DB_Connection {
    /* class definition */
}
```

If you define a class that executes an interface when in truth, it doesn't, you receive a compile-time error. Say, for example, you build a class DB_Foo that executes neither method:

```
<?php
require "DB/Connection.inc";
class DB_Foo implements DB_Connection {}
?>
```

If you execute the following class, it will generate this error:

```
Fatal error: Class db_foo contains 2 abstract methods and
must be declared abstract (db connection::execute, db
connection:: prepare)
in /Users/george/Advanced PHP/examples/chapter-2/14.php on
line 3
```

PHP does not allow multiple inheritances. In other words, a class cannot directly emerge from more than one class. For example, this is a wrong syntax:

```
class A extends B, C {}
```

But because an interface only defines a prototype and not an implementation, it is possible for a class to implement an arbitrary number of interfaces. Therefore, if you have two interfaces, you can choose to execute both of them as shown here:

```php
<?php
interface A {
    public function abba();
}
interface B {
    public function bar();
}
class C implements A, B {
    public function abba()
    {
        // abba;
    }
    public function bar()
    {
        // bar;
    }
}
?>
```

An intermediate process between interfaces and classes is the abstract classes. An abstract class can include fleshed-out methods and abstract methods. Here is an example of an abstract class A, which completely executes *abba ()* but interprets *bar ()* as an abstract.

```
abstract class A {
  public function abba()
  {
// abba
  }
abstract public function bar();
}
```

Since bar () has not been defined fully, it is hard for it to be instantiated. But a class can derive from it as long as the deriving class executes all of A's abstract methods. Next, it can be instantiated such that B extends A and executes bar (). This means it can be instantiated without much problem.

```
class B {
  public function bar()
  {
    $this->abba();
  }
}
$b = new B;
```

Since abstract classes execute some of their methods, they are also seen as classes from inheritance. In other words, a class can extend only a single abstract class.

Interfaces assist in preventing you from shooting yourself in the foot once you declare classes meant for polymorphic. However, they are half the answer to fixing delegation errors. You are also supposed to ensure that a function that expects an object to execute a particular interface acquires this object.

Of course, you can do this type of computation directly in your code by checking manually the class of the object using *is _ a ()* function:

```
function addDB($dbh)
{

if(!is_a($dbh, "DB_Connection")) {
  trigger_error("\$dbh is not a DB_Connection object", E_USER_ERROR);
  }
$this->dbh = $dbh;
}
```

This method has two drawbacks:

- It demands more verbiage to examine the type of passed parameter.

- Even more serious, it is not a member of the prototype declaration function. This implies that you cannot force this type of parameter evaluation in classes that run a specific interface.

PHP5 handles the following challenges by providing the alternative of type-checking function declarations and prototypes. To support this particular feature for a function, you can declare it as follows:

```
function addDB(DB_Connection $dbh)
{
   $this->dbh = $dbh;
}
```

This function works the same way as the previous one; it will display a fatal error if *$dbh* isn't an instance of the *DB_Connection* class.

The Factory pattern

This pattern creates a standard means for a class to build objects of other classes. The normal application of this is when you have a function that has to return objects of various classes based on the input parameters.

One of the biggest challenges in relocating services to a different database is identifying all the places where the old wrapper object is used and delivering the new one. Let us say you have a reporting database that is engraved in an Oracle database which you can access exclusively via a class known as *DB_Oracle_Reporting:*

197

```
class DB_Oracle_Reporting extends DB_Oracle { /* ... */}
```

The singleton pattern

One of the biggest problems with PHP4 is that it is difficult to execute singletons. The singleton pattern describes a class that contains a single global instance. There are a lot of places where singleton is the right choice. A user browsing only has a single set of cookies and only a single profile. In the same way, a class that encloses an HTTP request has only a single instance per request. If you include a database driver that doesn't share connections, you may decide to involve a singleton to make sure that only a single connection is open to a particular database at any given moment.

There are various methods you can use to apply singletons in PHP5. You can decide to declare all properties of an object as static, but that will build a strange syntax for handling the object, and you really don't use an instance of the object. Below is a simple class that can implement the Singleton pattern:

```php
<?php
class Singleton {
    static $property;
    public function __construct() {}
}

Singleton::$property = "foo";
?>
```

One powerful method you can use to run singletons in PHP5 is by using the factory method. This method creates a private reference to the first class of the instance and displays it on request. For example:

```
class Singleton {
  private static $instance = false;
  public $property;

private function _ _construct() {}
public static function getInstance()
{
  if(self::$instance === false) {
    self::$instance = new Singleton;
  }
return self::$instance;
  }
}

$a = Singleton::getInstance();
$b = Singleton::getInstance();
$a->property = "hello world";
print $b->property;
```

Running this particular program will display the message "hello world." But remember that the constructor in this program is private. Once a constructor is private, then you cannot create an instance using a new Singleton.

Chapter 3

Handling Errors

Errors are a must in programming. Errors in programming appear in two forms:

- External errors: These are errors that the code assumes an unanticipated path because of a section of the program not working as required. For instance, a database connection fails to be created when the code expects it to be created successfully in an external error.

- Code logic errors: These errors are typically known as bugs. They are the kind of errors that the design of the code is fundamentally flawed because of faulty logic or something simple like a typo.

These two types of errors have huge differences.

- External errors will always happen no matter how "bug-free" the code is. Keep in mind that there are no bugs inside because the code is external.

- Sometimes, external errors that are not considered in the code logic can become bugs. For instance, if you blindly assume that a database connection will always be established, it could be a bug because the application may fail to respond in the right way.

- The logic errors in the code are very difficult to trace than external errors because their location is not known. However, you can run data consistency tests to expose these errors.

PHP has built-in mechanisms to handle errors. Also, they have a built-in severity system that will let you identify only errors that are grave enough to raise your eyebrows. The main severity levels for PHP include:

```
•   E_NOTICE
•   E_WARNING
•   E_ERROR
```

Let us start with the **E_NOTICE**

It spots minor; nonfatal errors meant to help you locate possible bugs within your code. In general, an E_NOTICE error is something that functions but might not do what you want; for example, applying a variable in a non-assignment expression before it is assigned. Here is an example:

```php
<?php
$variable++;
?>
```

The above example will increase $variable to 1, but it will still show an E_NOTICE error. So you need to include:

```php
<?php
$variable = 0;
$variable++;
?>
```

This check is meant to restrict errors that may arise because of typos in the names of variables. For instance, this block of code will work well:

```php
<?
$variable = 0;
$variabel++;
?>
```

The $variable will not be incremented, but the $variable1 will be.

The E_NOTICE warning assists in capturing this type of error. It is the same as running a Perl program with *use warnings* and *use strict*.

In the PHP language, the errors from E_NOTICE are deactivated by default since they can generate a large and long repetitive log. However, it is good to turn it on for warning while writing programs so that you clean up your code. And remember to disable them once you launch your program on a production machine.

For the E_WARNING errors, they can be said to be nonfatal runtime errors. They don't stop or change the control flow of the code, but they will send an alert that something bad has happened. Most of the external errors produce E_WARNING errors. An example is receiving an error once you call *fopen()* to *mysql_connect ()*.

E_ERROR errors are the ones that you cannot recover and stop the implementation of the running program. Examples of the following errors are trying to instantiate a non-existent class.

PHP provides the function *trigger_error ()* that will let a user generate their own errors in a program.

A user can trigger three types of errors. These errors have a similar semantic to the one just discussed. Here is how you can trigger the errors:

```
while(!feof($fp)) {
  $line = fgets($fp);
  if(!parse_line($line)) {
    trigger_error("Incomprehensible data encountered", E_USER_NOTICE);
  }
}
```

In case the error level is not specified, the E_USER_NOTICE is applied.

Also, PHP has the E_ALL error type that handles all error reporting levels. You can regulate the level of errors that are produced in your code by applying the php.ini setting *error_reporting*.

Error_reporting includes the following for only fatal errors:

```
error_reporting = E_ERROR | E_USER_ERROR
```

Handle errors

Now that you know the type of errors that PHP will create, you need to set up a plan for handling them when they occur. PHP has four choices for dealing with errors that fall in the category of error_reporting:

- Display them

- Ignore them

- Log them

- Act on them

None of these choices is more important than the other. Each option has a significant place in the strong error-handling system. Outputting errors is crucial in a coding environment, and logging them is often the right thing in a production environment. Some errors require you to act on them, while others can be safely ignored.

The combination of the error-handling method you use depends on your preference and needs.

Display errors

If you choose to output errors in your program, the errors will be passed to the standard output stream. For those working in a webpage, the errors appear on the browser.

display_errors is important in programming because it ensures the developer received instant feedback on the problem that occurred on the script.

However, while the developer will understand these errors once they are displayed, the end user of the product tend to be frustrated when they come across these errors. Making your program to display PHP errors to your end users is not a good thing because:

- It sends a message to the end user that the site is buggy.

- It appears ugly.

- It can show details of the internal code that a user can apply for the wrong purpose.

If you want to verify whether your code has security holes for hackers to exploit, then you need to run in production using *display_errors* on.

So, you should turn on display errors in the process of development, but disable them during production.

Production display errors

The way to alert users of errors is always a huge debate. Most big clients have specific rules on what you need to do when a user finds an error. Certain business rules require the display of a customized theme too complex logic based on a cached type of the content they were searching for. From the point of business, this is reasonable: Your web availability is your vehicle to your customers, and any errors in it can change their perceptions of your entire business.

Irrespective of the exact content that requires to be returned to the user when an unexpected error happens, it is not good to reveal your debugging information to your users.

One of the most common methods used is to return a 500 error code from the page and define a custom error handler to redirect the user to a custom error page. In PHP, a 500 error code represents an internal server error. To display one from PHP language, you have to do the following:

```
header("HTTP/1.0 500 Internal Server Error");
```

Next, set the following in your apache configuration file:

```
ErrorDocument 500 /custom-error.php
```

This code will make any page to display a status code of 500 to be redirected to the user.

Logging errors

PHP language provides the ability to log to a file and log through syslog using two settings in the php.in file. This particular setting allows errors to be logged.

```
log_errors = On
```

Then the following two settings will make logging either to shift to a file or Syslog:

```
error_log = /path/to/filename
error_log = syslog
```

Logging generates a trace of any errors that occur on your website. When you fix a bug, you need to debug lines close to the area in question.

Besides the errors logged from system errors, you can manually trigger an error log message by including this particular line of code:

```
error_log("This is a user defined error");
```

Similarly, you can decide to send an email message. This is described in the PHP manual.

If you are working on a single server, you should access syslog file directly.

If you are working on multiple servers, you should limit excessive logging if you decide to use *syslog*.

Ignoring errors

PHP still presents you with an option to suppress the error reporting when you feel like it may happen. This is achieved using the @syntax. For that reason, if you want to open a file that may not exist and suppress the errors that emerge, you can apply the following syntax:

```php
$fp = @fopen($file, $mode);
```

Since PHP error mechanisms don't offer any flow control capability, you may choose to suppress errors that you feel may happen.

Take, for instance, a function that extracts the contents of a file that may not exist.

```php
$content = file_get_content($sometimes_valid);
```

If the file is not available, you will receive an E_WARNING error. If you believe this is an expected possible result, then you should consider suppressing this warning. You accomplish this by writing @operator, which will hide the warnings on individual calls:

```php
$content = @file_get_content($sometimes_valid);
```

Acting on errors

See the code below to learn how to set a custom error handler in PHP language:

```php
<?php
require "DB/Mysql.inc";
function user_error_handler($severity, $msg, $filename, $linenum) {
    $dbh = new DB_Mysql_Prod;
    $query = "INSERT INTO errorlog
                (severity, message, filename, linenum, time)
                VALUES(?,?,?,?, NOW())";
$sth = $dbh->prepare($query);
switch($severity) {
case E_USER_NOTICE:
    $sth->execute('NOTICE', $msg, $filename, $linenum);
    break;
case E_USER_WARNING:
    $sth->execute('WARNING', $msg, $filename, $linenum);
    break;
case E_USER_ERROR:
    $sth->execute('FATAL', $msg, $filename, $linenum);
    echo "FATAL error $msg at $filename:$linenum<br>";
    break;
default:
    echo "Unknown error at $filename:$linenum<br>";
    break;
    }
}
?>
```

You set a function this way:

```php
set_error_handler("user_error_handler");
```

If an error is found, instead of it being displayed on the screen, it is inserted into the database table of errors. And for fatal errors, a message is displayed on the screen. Remember that PHP error handlers don't create flow control. So if a nonfatal error happens when the processing is complete, the script resumes from the place where the error happens. But for fatal errors, the script will exit once the handler completes.

Send yourself an email

This can sound like a very good idea to notify yourself. You set in a custom error handler that has the mail () function to send an email to the developer. In general, this is not a great idea.

207

Why?

Errors tend accumulating. Please ensure that the error only occurs at most once per hour. However, if an unexpected error happens because of a bug in the code, you will receive multiple requests. In other words, your mailing error function may send over 20, 000 emails to your account even before you can turn it off. So you can see why it is not a good idea.

If you want to apply this type of reactive functionality in your error-handling program, it is better to write a script that will parse error logs and uses intelligent restriction to control the number of emails it can send.

Dealing with external errors

This chapter has been addressing error handling, while not much has been covered. So far, you know how to accept and process warning messages that your code can generate. However, one thing you haven't done is to use the methods to change the flow control in your code.

In reality, handling errors requires that you know exactly where code can break and choose what to do to fix that problem. External failures in a code happen due to connections or fetching data from an external process.

Let us look at this code written to return the *passwd* file details for a specific user:

```php
<?php
function get_passwd_info($user) {
    $fp = fopen("/etc/passwd", "r");
    while(!feof($fp)) {
        $line = fgets($fp);
        $fields = explode(";", $line);
        if($user == $fields[0]) {
            return $fields;
        }
    }
}
return false;
}
?>
```

As it is, the above code has two bugs.

First, there is a pure code logic, and secondly, there is a failure to account for a likely external error. If you run this program, it will output an array with elements this way:

```php
<?php
print_r(get_passwd_info('www'));
?>

Array
(
[0] => www:*:70:70:World Wide Web Server:/Library/WebServer:/noshell
)
```

And the reason is that the field separator inside the *passwd* file is:, and not;. As a result:

```
$fields = explode(";", $line);
needs to be this:
$fields = explode(":", $line);
```

The second bug is tiny. If you don't open the passwd file, you will trigger an E_WARNING error, but the flow of the program will continue. If a user does not exist in the passwd file, the function will output *false*. But suppose the *fopen* fails, the function also outputs false, which is now confusing.

This simple example illustrates one of the biggest problems that procedural languages have when it comes to error handling.

Exceptions

The methods reviewed so far were in existence before the release of PHP5, and you have seen that it creates big challenges, especially if you are working in a bigger application. The main drawback is displaying errors to a user of a library. Take, for instance, the error checking that you applied in the *passwd* file reading function.

When writing this example, you have two basic options of how you need to deal with a connection error:

- Deal with the error locally and display false data to the user.

- Propagate and retain the error, and display it to the caller rather than printing the result set.

For the passwd file reading example, you did not go with the first choice because it would be presumptuous for a library to be aware of the way the application requires it to fix the error.

The second method is not much better than the first because it requires one to have an eye for detail and proper planning to ensure errors can be propagated in the right way via an application.

For instance, if the result of the database is a string, how can you distinguish it with an error string?

Additional propagation has to be conducted manually. For every step, the error has to be manually sent to the caller and either passed along or fixed. This is more difficult to handle.

Well, exceptions have been developed to deal with this type of conditions. An exception is defined as a flow-control means that provides you with an option to disable the current program execution

210

and set the stack to a prescribed point. An object represents the error that occurs. This particular object is the exception.

In short, exceptions are just objects. PHP language contains a built-in Exception class that is meant specifically for exceptions. While it is not a must for exceptions to be an instance of the Exception class, there are advantages of having any class that you would like to throw exceptions coming from Exception.

To start a new Exception, you require to instantiate an instance of the Exception class you want, and then you throw it.

Once an exception is thrown, the object of the exception is saved, and the execution in the existing block of code stops immediately. In case there is an exception-handler block created in the existing block, the code moves to that location and implements the handler. If no handler is set in the existing scope, the stack of the implementation gets popped, and the scope of the caller is verified for an exception-handler block. This goes on until the time when the handler is located, or the main scope is attained.

If you execute the following code:

```php
<?php
throw new Exception;
?>
```

It will output the following:

```
> php uncaught-exception.php
Fatal error: Uncaught exception 'exception'! in Unknown on line 0
```

An exception that is not discovered results in a fatal error. Therefore, exceptions create their specific maintenance requirements. If you use exceptions as warnings in code, each caller in a block of code should be aware that an exception can be thrown and should be ready to deal with it.

Exception handling is made up of a block of statements you would like to try and a second block that you may want to enter if and when you spark errors. Below is an example that demonstrates how an exception is thrown and caught:

```
try {
    throw new Exception;
    print "This code is unreached\n";
}
catch (Exception $e) {
    print "Exception caught\n";
}
```

In the above example, an exception is thrown, but it is inside a try block, so execution stops and you move forward to catch block. *Catch* catches an Exception class so that a block is allowed. D catch is often used to execute any cleanup that may be relevant from the failure that happens.

Applying multiple Exception Hierarchies

It is possible to try numerous catch blocks if you would like to deal with different errors in a different way. For instance, you can change the factorial example so that it can deal with the case where $n is too big for PHP's math properties:

```php
class OverflowException {}
class NaNException {}
function factorial($n)
{
    if(!preg_match('/^\d+$/', $n) || $n < 0 ) {
        throw new NaNException;
    }

    else if ($n == 0 || $n == 1) {
        return $n;
    }
    else if ($n > 170 ) {
        throw new OverflowException;
    }
    else {
        return $n * factorial($n - 1);
    }
}
```

Now, you can deal with each error instance in a unique way.

```php
<?php
if($_POST['input']) {
    try {
        $input = $_POST['input'];
        $output = factorial($input);
        echo "$_POST[input]! = $output";
    }
    catch (OverflowException $e) {
        echo "The requested value is too large.";
    }
    catch (NaNException $e) {
        echo "Only natural numbers can have their factorial
            computed.";
    }
}
?>
```

As it is now, you need to enumerate each of the potential cases differently. This is both tiresome to write and possibly dangerous because as the library grows, the set of possible exceptions will increase, and this will make it easy to remove one accidentally.

To deal with this, you can categorize the exceptions together in families and develop an inheritance tree to connect them:

```
class MathException extends Exception {}
class NaNException extends MathException {}
class OverflowException extends MathException {}
```

Chapter 4

Running PHP-Templates
and the Web

O ne of the object-oriented programming properties that most people like to use in web programming is Model-View-Controller (MVC). MVC demands that an application should be divided into three parts:

- Model — The inner parts of a system that executes all the important business logic.

- View — The part that deals with formatting the system output.

- Controller — The part that processes input and sends it to the model.

The origin of MVC dates back to a Smalltalk paradigm for creating agile applications which a particular business process may have numerous methods for accepting data and displaying output.

Most web application accepts data only in a single approach, and at any time, the input processing is done using PHP. This excludes the fear of the controller component.

What is left after the controller is removed is the need to distinguish application logic from the output logic. This comes with several advantages:

- The application you build becomes more agile. A clear distinction allows you to easily alter the application logic or the external appearance of your pages without impacting the other.

- A clean code. Since you are forced to choose the application logic and output logic, your code will always look smarter.

- You can optimize the output code for reuse. The PHP code reuse is very common, but mixing your application code with the HTML makes it even difficult to reuse.

The application of MVC in the web environment is often made using templates. In a template structure, the HTML and output logic is kept in a *template*. The application code, which does not feature the output logic, parses the request and executes any needed task, and then sends the raw data to the template so that the template can prepare it ready for display.

There are many different types of array template solutions for PHP. This chapter will focus on Smarty, one of the most common and flexible template solutions. You will also learn how to use an ad hoc template just in case you don't prefer Smarty.

However, Smarty is simple. But as you begin to learn how to execute flow control, custom modifiers, custom functions, and the Smarty language can become complex. A designer that can manage to implement complex logic in Smarty can manage to do so in PHP language. And that is a good thing. Remember that PHP is a nice template language; it provides the tools to integrate formatting and output the logic into HTML.

If your environment has designers who are familiar to code in PHP and your whole team has the discipline enough to display logic differently, then a standard template language may not be relevant although it is rare to find designers who cannot handle PHP integration into their HTML. Still, if you are comfortable with PHP, template solutions are much better because they attempt to bring a distinction of output from application control.

Apart from building a standard difference between business logic and output logic, the correct justification for applying a template solution like Smarty is to provide untrusted end users the potential to create dynamic pages, without trusting them with access to PHP. This instance can occur in providing virtual storefronts or providing template solutions for creating emails.

Smarty

This is one of the most common and popularly used template systems in PHP. It is a flexible and fast template to support the separation of application and output logic. It operates by picking special markup in template files and processing it into a cached PHP script. This compilation is open and makes the system fast.

How to install smarty

In general, it has a set of PHP classes, and you can find it online at **https://www.smarty.net/.** If you use PEAR, it is better to install Smarty into the PEAR include path. Smarty isn't a project of PEAR, so you should not fear if you place it in the PEAR hierarchy.

You will have to download Smarty and copy all the libraries of Smarty into a PEAR subdirectory.

Next, you will have to create directories from which Smarty can access its configuration and template files. Again, you will need to create a path where Smarty can write the processed template and cached files.

Smarty natively includes two levels of caching into its design. The first design is when the template is viewed, Smarty will process it into pure PHP and save the result. This process of caching will restrict the template tags from the need for compilation once the first request is over. Secondly, Smarty will support optional caching of the initial printed content.

The web server implements processed templates and cache files as the templates are first accessed, so the directories should be writable by the user that web server operates. For security reasons, your web server should not alter files stored in the *ServerRoot*. So you should have the directories placed in a separate tree.

The simplest way to notify Smarty of the location of these directories is by extending the base Smarty class for each application that will use it.

The first Smarty template

You will change the following PHP page into a template.

```
<html>
<body>
Hello <?php
if(array_key_exists('name', $_GET)) {
    echo $_GET['name'];
else {
    echo "Stranger";
}
?>
</body>
</html>
```

The location for this template will be:

```
/data/www/www.example.org/templates/
hello.tpl
```

And it will appear this way:

```
<html>
<body>
Hello {$name}
</body>
</html>
```

By default, the specific tags for Smarty are surrounded in brackets ({}).

The PHP page *hello.php* file that uses the following template appears this way:

```
require_once 'Smarty_ExampleOrg.php'; // Your Specialized
Smarty Class
$smarty = new Smarty_ExampleOrg;
$name = array_key_exists('name', $_COOKIE) ? $_COOKIE[
'name'] : 'Stranger';
$smarty->assign('name', $name);
$smarty->display('index.tpl');
```

Notice that the $name inside the template and that $name in the hello.php are different. To fill $name within the template, you will have to allocate it to the Smarty scope by doing the following:

```
$smarty->assign('name', $name);
```

Smarty control structures

By applying simple variable substitution, it makes Smarty appear powerful. Your templates look simple and clean, and the back-end code is pretty simple too.

The first problem you may experience while implementing any template structure is creating tables and conditionally displaying the data.

In case a registered person of your site accesses hello.php, you may want to print a link to the login page for that person. You have two choices. The first one is to extract the logic into the PHP code, as follows:

```
/* hello.php */
$smarty = new Smarty_ExampleOrg;
$name = array_key_exists('name', $_COOKIE) ? $_COOKIE[
'name'] : 'Stranger';
if($name == 'Stranger') {
  $login_link = "Click <a href=\"/login.php\">here</a> to
  login.";
} else {
$login_link = '';
}
$smarty->assign('name', $name);
$smarty->assign('login_link', $login_link);
$smarty->display('hello.tpl');
```

Smarty Functions and More

Besides the basic flow control, Smarty allows a person to call built-in and user-defined functions. This will enhance the flexibility of what you can manage with the template code itself, but you will need to make the template complex.

The most relevant built-in function is **include**. This is analogous to the include () function in PHP; the Smarty function permits you to include another template. The most common application for this is to include headers and footers in their specific **includes,** as shown below:

```
{* header.tpl *}
<html>
<head>
    <title>{$title}</title>
{if $css}
<link rel="stylesheet" type="text/css" href="{$css}" />
{/if}
</head>
<body>
{* footer.tpl *}
<!-- Copyright &copy; 2003 George Schlossnagle. Some rights
reserved. -->
</body>
</html>
```

Therefore, any template that will require headers and footers, you will need to include them this way:

```
{* hello.tpl *}
{include file="header.tpl"}
Hello {$name}.
{include file="footer.tpl"}
```

Smarty will also allow the PHP function, which enables PHP to be inlined within the template. This will permit you to run something like this:

220

```
{* hello.tpl *}
{include file="header.tpl"}
Hello {php}print $_GET['name'];{/php}
{include file="footer.tpl"}
```

Caching using smarty

Quicker than applying compiled versions of templates is caching the display of templates so that the template does not require any execution. As a whole, caching is a powerful feature. To cache something in Smarty, you will need to enable the caching inside the class using this line:

```
$smarty->cache = true;
```

Now, if you make a call to display (), the whole output of the page is going to be cached. In most pages, the most expensive section occurs in the PHP code, where you need to set up the data to generate the page. If you don't want to follow this process, you can apply the method is_cached () to determine if a cached copy is available. Within your PHP code, this would be applied as follows:

```
$smarty = new Smarty_ExampleOrg;
if(!is_cached('index.tpl')) {
    /* perform setup */
}
$smarty->display('index.tpl');
```

In case your page contains personalized information, this is not what you wish for because it will cache the first user's personalized information and serve that to subsequent users.

If you would like to cache the data conditionally, you can decide to pass a second parameter into the output function. This will make the caching system to apply that as a key to display the cached content to a different request.

Chapter 5

PHP Standalone Scripts

There are several advantages of an extremely specialized language, and these are:

- It is easy to use as it is the best tool for a particular job if you are appointed to perform the job.

- It is easy to work in a niche than to compete with other general purpose languages.

Likewise, there are disadvantages of highly specialized languages like:

- Companies don't concentrate on a single niche to the removal of all others.

- Fulfilling different needs with specialist languages means developers need to master more than one language.

- A common code is duplicated in every language applied.

- If you are a web expert, you need to turn these problems into serious challenges.

A duplicated code implies that bugs have to be fixed in more than one place, which means there will be a higher bug rate and behavior for bugs to remain on lesser used sections of code. Actively building code in different languages implies that developers don't become experts in one language; they need to know many languages. This makes it difficult to have expert programmers because their focus is divided between many languages. Similarly, some good companies deal with this problem by creating different groups of programmers who deal with specific business sides. While this can be effective, it does not provide the answer to the code-reuse problem. In fact, it is expensive and limits the agility of the business.

Experience shows that the perfect language features a specialist-like affinity for the main focus of your projects, but still, it can handle peripheral tasks that emerge. For most of the web-programming requirements, PHP is a suitable candidate. The PHP development structure has remained disciplined to its web-scripting roots. PHP language has also met the needs of general problems. As a result, PHP has fulfilled different non-web programming needs.

PHP command-line interface

The PHP script is executed on the command line with the help of a Unix system. You type the following code:

> php phpscript.php

For Windows systems, the registry will be altered to identify Php scripts using PHP executable so that once you click on them, they will be parsed and executed.

Apart from how they deal with input, the PHP command-line scripts behave similarly like the web-based systems.

Chapter 6

Controlling the Development Environment

For most developers, maintaining a massive software project is one of the least interesting parts of the job.

Unlike the agile web development model where changes occur rapidly, project management is usually about placing a throttle on development efforts to uphold quality control.

Enterprise is a hyped word used to refer to the software. Enterprise software can be described as an important part of a business. In the software environment, the term enterprise is used to refer to more properties:

- Scalable

- Robust

- Adaptable

- Secure

- Well-tested

- Professional

It is difficult to measure any of the above qualities quantitatively, but they appear like something that any business owner may want to have. So it would be crazy if a business owner rejects an enterprise software.

The challenge with enterprise is that it offers room for people to market their software as the perfect solution for any problem without demonstrating why it is better than others. The qualities mentioned previously are important if you are expanding business around software.

There are two features of management:

- **Change control**. This involves handling any site, whether large or small, without having an established change control system.

- **Managing Packaging**. This is closely similar to change control. Controlling the package ensures that you can move site versions forward and backward and in a distributed environment.

Change control

The change control software describes a tool that lets you monitor individual changes to project files and develop project versions that are related to specific file versions. This ability is important in the software development process because you can track and revert changes. You don't have to recall why you performed a certain change or what the code appeared like before you implemented a change. By looking at the differences between file versions, you can tell when a change occurred, identify the differences, and determine why the change was done.

So far, the open-source standard that supports change control is the Concurrent Versioning System (CVS).

CVS

This isn't the only versioning standard available. There are many options to CVS. However, CVS has widely been used as a change control system; hence, the one that you are likely to come across.

Using CVS

Some people build software without providing room for change control. Keep in mind that change control is a vital feature of programming. Even when you write your personal projects, you should not forget to use CVS.

The first step to control files using CVS is to extract a project into a CVS repository. To develop a local repository, you need to build a directory where all the repository files will remain. You can name this path as /var/CVS, but any other path will still work. Since this is a permanent repository for your project data, you need to store your repository in a place that it will be backed up regularly. First, you define the base directory and then use CVS init to create the base directory:

```
> mkdir /var/cvs
> cvs -d /var/cvs init
```

Altering files

Now, let us assume that you have extracted all your files into CVS, and you have applied some changes. When you modify files in your working directory, there will be no interruption with the master repository that will take place. Once you confirm that you are okay with the changes, you can allow CVS to commit the changes to the master repository. Once you do that, your changes will remain permanent in the repository.

Allowing multiple developers to work on the same project

One of the major problems experienced in letting many people work to make changes to the same file actively is compiling the changes so that the work of one developer does not override the other one. CVS has the update functionality to make this possible. You can use this functionality in different ways. The easiest way is to attempt to ensure that a file is up-to-date.

Chapter 7

Designing a Great API

What makes a certain code good and another one bad? If the code works well and has no bugs, can that code be said to be good? Not really.

Every code will come to live past its initial application, and hence, if you want to assess its quality, you need to consider the following:

- Is it easy to reuse in different contexts?

- Is it easy to maintain?

- Does it have the least external dependencies?

This list can further be categorized into the following three parts:
- Has to be refactored

- Has to be written defensively

- Has to be extensible

Bottom-up and top-bottom

When it comes to software development, the design is an important stage.

Design is divided into bottom-up and top-down.

The bottom-up design is one where the code is written early in the development cycle. In this particular design, the low-level parts are developed first.

Some things to note about bottom-up is that:

- It provides quick deliverables.

- It is not hard to deal with changes in design.

One of the disadvantages of bottom-up design is that the low-level parts are compiled and the external APIs go through rapid and quick change. In other words, while you start to build the project early, the end is filled with a lot of redesigns.

However, when it comes to the top-down design, the entire application is divided into subsystems. Next, the subsystems are divided into components. Until the whole system has been designed is the only time when functions and classes can be implemented.

Some of the advantages of top-down design include:

- You acquire a robust API early.

- You are guaranteed that all the parts will fit together. This means that there will be minimal reengineering required.

The design for refactoring and extensibility

It is so surprising to many developers that it is okay to have a poorly implemented code with a robust API design than have a well-implemented code that has a poor API design. Your code will indeed live on, be reused, and acquire a life of its own. If the design of your API is good, then it is easy for the code to be refactored to optimize the performance. On the other hand, if the API design library is poor, any changes that you apply have to be cascaded to all the code that uses it.

Writing code that is easy to change is important to ensure that you have a code that is reusable and easy to maintain. Well, how can you design code so that it can be easy to refactor later?

Here are some of the features to consider:

- Limit interdependencies in your code.

- Encapsulate the logic inside the functions.

- Ensure that classes and functions are simple

- Apply a namespacing approach to compartmentalize your code.

Conclusion

You have just had a bird's eye view of what is described as an advanced PHP for web development.

PHP is not designed only for professional web developers, neither do you need to be an IT professional. Like any other scripting language, PHP can appear complicated at first glance. But if you can persevere, you will discover that this is an exciting language. It is also a better means of gaining knowledge of the server-side world.

Some people may tell you that you need to understand one thing fully before you can move to the next. Well, being determined to learn something is a good thing. There's no argument there but with a big BUT. The but is that it is good to reread everything you study at least twice. So you are going to be back here anyway. You need to look at the real learning process in a long-term way, not just short-term where you read it once and understood everything. That rarely happens.

So if you want to make the best out of this PHP book, you should consider reading it at least twice. That way, you will be building a general understanding of the landscape you are handling. And this is what is referred to as the "general to specific" learning approach. So once you develop that birds-eye-view framework, you can dive deeper and learn the specifics of PHP. This is true because it will allow you to see how things compile. You will be able to see the practical application of things.

Description

D o you want to take your web dev skills to the next level? Discover the power of PHP as you take your web development skills to the next level. PHP is the most common programming language for server-side web development. One of the best things about this language is that it is fairly easy to learn. In fact, most beginners find the language simple.

This books takes you through the advanced parts of the PHP server-side language, including abstract classes, extend interfaces, object-oriented programming, and many more. You will learn an overview of each topic, teach you how to code each item, and then show you how to expand further.

Discover how to solve problems, establish consistency, and prevent your program from crashing by using the techniques shared in this book. Take your object-oriented programming skills beyond the basics and methods into implementing constructors, destructors, and singletons. Learn how to create exceptions, and explore more ways you can build a flexible software using PHP.

Topics include:

- Design patterns

- Building a great API

- PHP coding styles

- Smarty templates

- Object-oriented programming

- And many more.

Are you ready to launch your PHP coding skills to the next level?

52238662R00131

Made in the USA
Lexington, KY
10 September 2019